SpringerBriefs in Digital Spaces

Series editor

Ahmed Bounfour, Orsay, France

For further volumes:
http://www.springer.com/series/10461

Kai Reimers · Xunhua Guo
Mingzhi Li · Bin Xie · Tiantian Zhang

Innovating in a Learning Community

Emergence of an Open Information Infrastructure in China's Pharmaceutical Distribution Industry

Springer

Kai Reimers
Tiantian Zhang
School of Business and Economics
RWTH Aachen University
Aachen
Germany

Xunhua Guo
Mingzhi Li
Bin Xie
School of Economics and Management
Tsinghua University
Beijing
China

ISSN 2193-5890 ISSN 2193-5904 (electronic)
ISBN 978-3-319-05097-3 ISBN 978-3-319-05098-0 (eBook)
DOI 10.1007/978-3-319-05098-0
Springer Cham Heidelberg New York Dordrecht London

Library of Congress Control Number: 2014932970

Printed on acid-free paper

Springer is part of Springer Science+Business Media (www.springer.com)

Contents

Introduction

How do firms jointly develop open information infrastructures? As industry-wide information infrastructures become crucial facilitators for improved supply chain management as well as for novel services, the question of how such infrastructures develop or, rather, evolve becomes practically relevant. Special interest will focus on whether such infrastructures will be open or, in contrast, will become the means of market closure and market power. To answer this question, we draw on the results of a longitudinal research project covering the development of the pharmaceutical distribution industry in China from 2004 to 2012, focusing on the emergence and subsequent evolution of industry-wide information infrastructures.

The pharmaceutical distribution industry in China provides an ideal setting for understanding the long-term emergence and evolution of an industry-wide information infrastructure. The time span over which infrastructure development occurs is more compressed in China as, on the one hand, it only recently embarked on a far-reaching societal modernization process and, on the other hand, proceeds through the several development stages much more rapidly than elsewhere. Thus, evolutionary processes occur in relatively shorter time periods than elsewhere and, therefore, are more accessible to a systematic research study. Moreover, the Chinese government is paying considerable attention to the use of information technology in China's pharmaceutical distribution industry since it is expected that required and desired organizational and institutional change will be facilitated if accompanied by implementation of modern information technologies. Thus, the development process is driven by specific government objectives under conditions of a supposedly powerful government. Studying information infrastructure development in this context should reveal the possibilities and limitations of purposefully steering the development process.

To facilitate our analytical task, we break down our overall research question—How do firms jointly develop open information infrastructures—into a number of sub-questions more limited in their scope, namely: How do firms delimit areas of proprietary innovation in open innovation projects? How do firms coordinate (initiate, negotiate, implement) the development of innovative infrastructures? How do processes and practices within firms enable and constrain such collective efforts? Do collective infrastructure projects give rise to specific industry-level practices that have their own rules, norms and ideational structures? If so, how do such emergent practices, in turn, constrain and enable activities by individual firms?

Development of open information infrastructures has not only effects at the industry level with implications for policy makers but will also pose new challenges and opportunities for companies. We will therefore also derive implications for management in the context of the discussion about the 'Enterprise 2020'.

The argument progresses in two steps which correspond to two questions that structured our research process: (1) What drives the emergence of an industry-wide information infrastructure? (2) How does an emerging industry-wide information infrastructure further develop once in existence? Based on the insights and empirical findings that we obtained with respect to these two analytical steps we will then address the research questions given above in the conclusions and also expand on the managerial implications of our findings.

While our study focuses on the evolution of platforms used for managing commercial transactions across the pharmaceutical supply chain, there were other important developments contributing to the overall industry-wide information infrastructure that provided the context for our study and occasionally interacted with developments that were the focus of our study. For example, systems for managing commercial transactions generally greatly benefit from the availability of standardized product names and codes. These, in turn, are important in other systems as well such as Electronic Patient Records (EPR) and systems for tracking and tracing drugs to ensure drug safety. We have therefore compiled a separate account of EPR systems and tracking and tracing technologies to provide a critical context for our data analysis and interpretation. Since this is the first English language account of these developments in China we make it available to the interested reader as an appendix to our study.

Chapter 1
A Simple Theoretical Framework

Understanding the long-term development of industry-wide information infrastructures (III) is a challenge that has not yet been sufficiently addressed in the literature. The Chinese context provides an ideal setting to study III emergence because of initially low levels of computer use and also because the development unfolds more rapidly than is usual in other national environments. Against this setting, we deemed a life cycle approach to understanding III emergence especially promising since it potentially accounts for all phases of III emergence and also suggests a succession of these phases, thus offering the promise of limited predictive power.

For this purpose, we draw on a previously developed multi-level framework to explain the emergence of B2B electronic commerce, here interpreted as an information infrastructure (Reimers et al. 2004). This framework uses established theories of organizational and industry life cycles to argue that the conditions for B2B electronic commerce to emerge involve maturity on both levels, the industry and the organizational level. This framework is used to derive operational indicators of company and industry maturity. These indicators then provide a theoretical scaffolding for coding our data.

In our earlier paper (Reimers et al. 2004) we built a comprehensive argument for a multi-level approach towards understanding the emergence of information infrastructures. Here, we briefly introduce the model to the extent that is necessary to understand our analytic and coding method while we have to refer the interested reader to our earlier paper for a discussion and selection of the relevant theories and their critiques which have been formulated in the literature.

Regarding the company level, Nolan and colleagues (Nolan 1973; Nolan et al. 1993) have argued that firms have to learn how to effectively use successive waves of new information technologies and distinguish between four learning stages which, according to the authors, can be measured by the growth of the IT budget of a company. Nolan (1973) proposes four indicators, so-called growth processes, to measure a company's progression in its IT learning process: the structure of the application portfolio, the nature of the IT resource, the type of management control, and the degree of user awareness. Nolan et al. (1993) further distinguish between three so-called eras characterized by three underlying technologies

K. Reimers et al., *Innovating in a Learning Community*, SpringerBriefs in Digital Spaces,
DOI: 10.1007/978-3-319-05098-0_1, © The Author(s) 2014

Table 1.1 Industry life cycle characteristics according to the models by Klepper and Graddy (1990); Utterback and Abernathy (1975) and Abernathy and Utterback (1978)

	Product characteristics	Innovation focus	No. of firms	Horizontal relationships	Vertical relationships
Growth stage	High degree of variety in terms of product design	Product	Initially small, then rising rapidly	Competition based on product innovation; cooperation on joint standards	Depends upon the type of companies dominating the industry (start-ups vs. established)
Shake-out stage	A common design—so-called dominant design—has emerged	Production process	Falling sharply	Hostile and desperate, struggle for survival; cooperation in order to join forces (Bertrand competition)	Competition for total value added; pressure on supply chain partners to cut costs
Stable stage	Dominant design persists	Production process	Stabilizing on low level	Oligopolistic competition based on process innovation; extensive cooperation with competitors in areas of common concerns	Forging of linkages to create integrated supply chains

(in brackets): data processing era (mainframe computing), micro era (micro and personal computers), and network era (data communication networks). Accordingly, companies can be classified in terms of how far they have advanced in their learning and technology absorption process with regard to each era.

On the industry level, the concept of the industry life cycle has originally been introduced by Utterback and Abernathy (Utterback and Abernathy 1975; Abernathy and Utterback 1978) and was later extended based on systematic empirical studies of industry evolution which revealed a surprising regularity in terms of the number of firms in an industry over time (Klepper and Graddy 1990). Authors have used different ways to describe this pattern by dividing it into two, three and four phases. Here, we rely on the phase scheme proposed by Klepper and Graddy (1990) which distinguishes between three phases, namely growth, shake-out and stable stage. Table 1.1 summarizes industry characteristics for these three stages.

In our model, we further distinguish between industry development of provider and user industries, arguing that development and use of new technologies are not necessarily synchronized. We then integrate these three levels (provider industry level, user industry level, and user company level) by mapping the several development or life cycles onto one another, as shown in Fig. 1.1. Essentially, we argue that for III to emerge companies must have mastered network-era

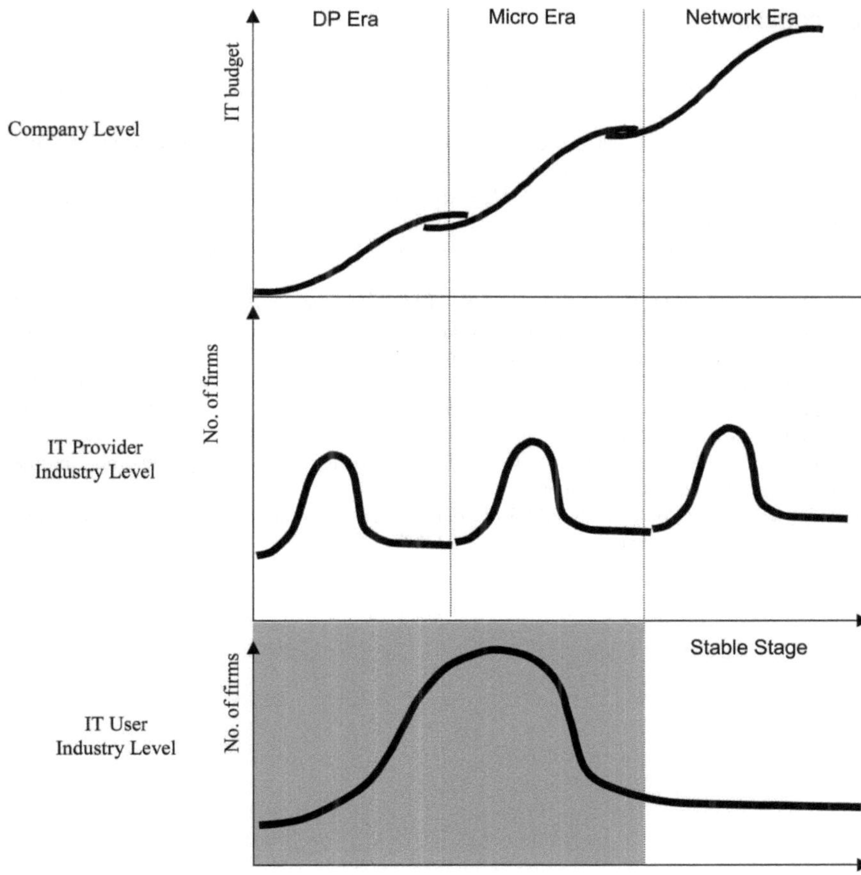

Fig. 1.1 Integrating three levels of development cycles (*Source* Reimers et al. 2004)

technology, the IT provider industry must offer network era products and services and the IT user industry must have reached the stable, third stage.

In addition, in our coding we have also allowed for categories to emerge in a bottom-up way (Neuman 2000). In an iterative manner involving interpretation of codes against possible theories and going back to the interview transcripts, we finally classified these emergent codes as expressing intended and unintended effects of government action as well as the institutional context of the case. According to Van de Ven and Poole (1995), organizational change theories based on intended and unintended effects can be categorized as a teleological theories since the phenomenon is explained in view of the objectives of certain strategically positioned actors. We thus use two broad approaches to code and interpret our data which we call a life cycle and a teleological approach.

References

Abernathy, W. J., & Utterback, J. M. (1978). Patterns of industrial innovation. *Technology Review, 80*(7), 40–47.

Klepper, S., & Graddy, E. (1990). The evolution of new industries and the determinant of market structure. *Rand Journal of Economics, 21*(1), 27–44.

Neuman, W. L. (2000). *Social Research Methods: Qualitative and Quantitative Approaches* (4th ed.). Boston: Allyn and Bacon.

Nolan, R. L. (1973). Managing the computer resource: A stage hypothesis. *Communications of the ACM, 16*(7), 399–405.

Nolan, R. L., Croson, D. C., & Seger, K. N. (1993). *The stages theory: a framework for IT adoption and organizational learning*, (Harvard Business School Note, No. 9-193-141). Boston: Harvard Business School Publishing.

Reimers, K., Li, M., & Chen, G. (2004). A multi-level approach for devising effective B2B E-commerce development strategies with an application to the case of China. *Electronic Commerce Research, 4*(3), 287–305.

Utterback, J. M., & Abernathy, W. J. (1975). A dynamic model of process and product innovation. *Omega, 3*(6), 639–656.

Van de Ven, A. H., & Poole, M. S. (1995). Explaining development and change in organizations. *Academy of Management Review, 20*(3), 510–540.

Chapter 2
Method

The study, which commenced in 2004 and is still ongoing, is supported by a research environment that we call a Learning Community (LC). This is a novel concept and research tool that comprises an industry group which engages in collective action to create a novel information infrastructure. 'Industry group' is defined in terms of a value system which includes all value activities that are needed to provide a particular product or service, in this case the provisioning of pharmaceutical products to the population. This typically includes hospitals, manufacturers, pharmacies and various intermediaries such as wholesalers/distributors, logistics firms and others such as e-commerce intermediaries. The Learning Community is used to validate and extend results from interviews that were conducted between 2004 and 2012 and that constitute the main empirical basis for this study.

Our research collaboration in general and the Learning Community environment in particular were used to answer the research questions outlined above that constitute the subject of this book. The overall research collaboration is broader in focus and the Learning Community may be viewed as a kind of field laboratory which supports several study projects to be conducted simultaneously. Thus, the study, the results of which are reported here, is embedded in this larger effort. In the following we will refer to this more narrow study simply as 'the project' defined by our research purpose as given above.

Our research question was to be answered in several steps. Specifically, two joint discussions and meetings among the involved researchers were to be arranged to coincide with the bi-annual workshops that take place as part of the Learning Community (LC) project (in May and November respectively). Moreover, further discussions and collaborations were undertaken for mutual extended visits. The first meeting in Beijing on the occasion of the LC workshop in November 2011 was used to discuss and determine the range of theories to be used for our project. A research stay of Prof. Xunhua Guo in Aachen was devoted to discussing intermediate results. An extended research stay of Prof. Kai Reimers in Beijing in May 2012, which coincided with a congregation of the Learning Community on May 25, was used to further discuss our intermediate findings and to set up a process for rigorously coding our data. Prof. Bin Xie visited Aachen in the summer of 2012 to further discuss our findings and interpretations. Moreover, the research

K. Reimers et al., *Innovating in a Learning Community*, SpringerBriefs in Digital Spaces,
DOI: 10.1007/978-3-319-05098-0_2,

team has held weekly teleconference meetings throughout the period of study to facilitate a joint interpretation and common conclusion of our results.

Our main research method was a longitudinal case study of an emerging information infrastructure within the Chinese pharmaceutical distribution industry. This covered the period from 2004 to 2012 and involved interviews, meetings with industry participants, and the workshops of our Learning Community (from 2009 onwards). In addition, content analysis of published documents was performed. This mostly referred to rules, guidelines, and laws issued by several government agencies. In total, 48 documents about interviews, meetings, and workshops were carefully coded and tabulated.

The unit of analysis is China's market for pharmaceutical distribution comprising all distribution stages and relevant organizations (as described below) over the period of observation (2004 to 2012).

Interviewees covered all relevant actors in the industry; specifically, they included wholesaler-distributors (the top three distributors in Beijing), retailers, manufacturers, e-commerce intermediaries, third party logistics service providers (3PLs), hospitals, trade associations, a leading trade magazine, government agencies (including the Ministry of Health and the State Food and Drug Administration, SFDA), a government body responsible for the centralized bidding system in Beijing, and a prominent individual in the industry who was instrumental in implementing an e-commerce initiative of central government.

We conducted two kinds of analyses. First, we constructed a time line of government actions concerning the industry in general and information infrastructure development in particular. Second, we coded our primary data according to our theoretical framework. Specifically, we derived indicators for company level development as well as for industry level development as defined by the life cycle theories from which we constructed our framework as described above. We then carefully read all transcripts and interview minutes and extracted statements that pertained to our indicators. All these statements were recorded in a spreadsheet. In addition, we allowed further indicator categories to emerge which we ultimately labelled intended and unintended effects of government action and institutional context. Subsequently, we prepared a synthesis for each indicator based on all the extracted statements pertaining to that indicator. The detailed results of our data analysis are contained in Appendix I. We have also compiled a timeline of government actions as a separate narrative (see Appendix II). This gives a detailed account of government actions focussing on the introduction of Electronic Patient Records (EPR) and Tracking & Tracing technologies. While these technologies are different from the electronic bidding platform discussed here, the evolution of EPRs and the tracking infrastructure creates the background against which government and firms were discussing and responding to the electronic bidding initiatives. This appendix can be read as a complementary text to our study here or, alternatively, as a separate text if one is predominantly interested in how the informatization of the healthcare and pharmaceutical industry in China proceeded in general.

For our discussion, we also rely on findings from our earlier study (Reimers et al. 2004) in which we developed our multi-level approach as well as collected some first data concerning firms and industries in China. Specifically, we found in that earlier study that the IT provider industry in China generally was able to offer network era products and services. We concluded that the IT provider industry did not represent a significant bottleneck for information infrastructure emergence and therefore did not analyse our data for evidence regarding the development stage of the IT provider industry but relied on these earlier results for an estimate.

Reference

Reimers, K., Li, M., & Chen, G. (2004). A multi-level approach for devising effective B2B E-commerce development strategies with an application to the case of China. *Electronic Commerce Research, 4*(3), 287–305.

Chapter 3
Historical Context and Precedents

In the early 2000s, amid the difficulties facing the overall medical and healthcare industry, the chaotic situation in the pharmaceutical distribution chain triggered the government to centralize drug procurement on the national level, based on electronic biddings systems. To put this policy in perspective, China's pharmaceutical distribution system has gone through four stages of dramatic changes, dating back to the planned economy era. In this chapter, we give a brief account of the history of China's pharmaceutical distribution industry including the precedents of its emerging information infrastructure in order to provide the context for our data analysis.

3.1 Three-Tier System of Drug Distribution in the Planned Economy Era (Before Mid 1980s)

Before China started economic reform in the 1980s, pricing and delivery of drugs were tightly controlled by the government through a three-tier distribution system (see Fig. 3.1). All medicines were distributed from several government-controlled regional wholesalers (first tier wholesalers) to provincial level wholesalers (second-tier wholesalers) who would then distribute the medicines to third-tier city level or county level local drug wholesalers. Retailers, including hospitals, clinics and pharmacies, ordered medicines through the third-tier wholesalers.

3.2 Deregulating the Drug Distribution Industry (Mid 1980s to 1999)

This three-tier drug distribution system was characterized by a lack of efficiency due to the existence of multiple intermediaries. Since the mid 1980s, government loosened its control over the system and allowed private firms to enter the industry,

K. Reimers et al., *Innovating in a Learning Community*, SpringerBriefs in Digital Spaces,
DOI: 10.1007/978-3-319-05098-0_3,

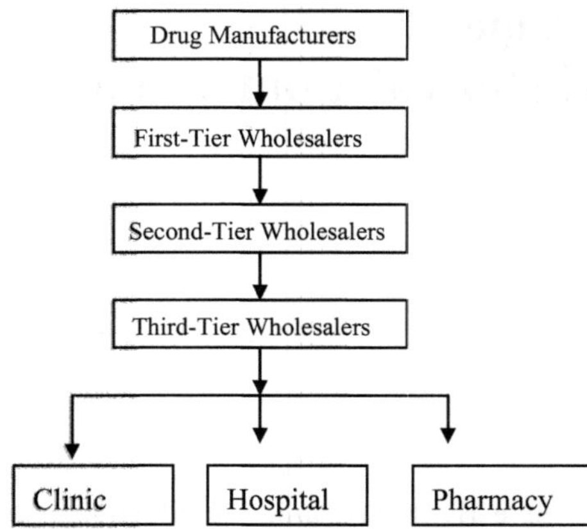

Fig. 3.1 The three-tier structure of drug distribution in China's planned economy era

and the planned economy era's rigid medicine distribution system was gradually phased out. By the end of the 1990s, the drug distribution industry was highly fragmented, with more than 16,000 firms of a variety of sizes in business. With the opening up of the markets and the deregulation of prices, drug prices increased dramatically which caused great public dissatisfaction.

One of the major reasons for the current market structure are the loopholes in the government's drug approval process. For years, China's pharmacies and hospitals have been plagued by low quality and faked medicine made by local drug companies. In recent years there have been several publicized cases in which patients were poisoned or even killed by these types of drugs. The fear is that lax government oversight is allowing drug companies to cut corners or circumvent safety procedures.

3.3 Government's Efforts of Centralizing the Drug Distribution Process (2000–2010)

In the year 2000, the State Planning Committee issued a document "on the reforming of managing the drug prices" which built a foundation for the government's regulation of drug prices. Together with other legal rules titled "the Price Law", "Drugs Regulation Law", and "Rules for Regulating Drug Prices", a set of government regulations was put in place. Meanwhile, the government decided to tighten its control over the drug distribution process and to implement the policy of centralized drug procurement. Although the Ministry of Health had issued some guidelines for the centralized drug procurement procedure, different regions had substantial flexibility in practice. Despite the differences in the procedures implemented in different regions, results showed unanimously that the centralized bidding and procurement practices didn't meet original goals set by the government. Among all the reasons, the additional charges imposed by the new bidding platforms were often cited as the most pertinent one for the resistance from the trading parties.

3.4 Latest Development: The Government Takes Over the Pharmaceutical Bidding and Procurement Process (Since Late 2010)

On November 19, 2010, the State Council of China issued the "Guidelines for Establishing and Normalizing the Mechanism of Essential Drug Procurement in Medical Institutions Run by the Government," which marks the abandonment of the third party electronic intermediary platforms. In this document, it is stipulated that the government will intensify the national essential drug system and the province-level medical administrative bureaus will be the sole responsible entity and carrier of the centralized essential drug bidding and procurement practice while the city level and below are not allowed to operate bidding and procurement platforms or assign procurement organizations. The essential drug bidding and procurement platforms are defined as not for profit organizations run by the government, which will be funded from the government budget and no charges should be levied on either the drug manufacturers or medical service institutions. In principle, medicines in huge demand will be procured directly from the manufacturers who are responsible for delivering the products or assigning distributors to fulfil the task, and the ones with small demand can be aggregated in batch and ordered from pharmaceutical distributors. Another important rule in the national essential drug system is the zero mark-up policy, i.e., the price charged to the patients by the hospitals will be the same as the procurement price (plus logistics costs).

Chapter 4
Summary of Data Analysis

As described above, we have used two approaches to analyse our data, which we labelled a life cycle and a teleological approach. The life cycle approach is based on our previously published multi-level framework for studying the emergence of B2B e-commerce systems and the teleological approach is based on a bottom-up coding process.

The multilevel framework describes several indicators to asses the degree of maturity on the organizational and the industry level respectively. For the industry level, these are:

- Dominant design: has a dominant design emerged that describes the main characteristics of the product? In service industries, the dominant design can be conceptualised as the dominant business model of providers.
- Number of firms: it has been found that the industry life cycle can be reliably measured by the development of the number of firms over time. After an initial period of experimentation with only a few active participants, this number rises dramatically as the new industry develops a successful product and thus provides growing profit opportunities; once a dominant design has emerged, competition centres on process innovations, leading to a dramatic shake out since economies of scale become dominant. After this, the industry enters a phase of stability with an oligopolistic structure.
- Process versus product innovation: related to the concept of dominant design, this indicator suggests that companies will shift their focus from product to process innovations once a dominant design (or a dominant business model) has emerged.
- Vertical linkages: as firms that have survived the shake-out phase are firmly established, it becomes possible to develop intensely cooperative relations with customers (vertical linkages) since competition focuses on value added services, such as just-in-time delivery, rather than price and quality.
- Horizontal linkages: relations among competitors (horizontal linkages) become more cooperative in this stable phase as competitors need to agree on a range of issues of common concern, including standards, for example in the area of e-commerce.

K. Reimers et al., *Innovating in a Learning Community*, SpringerBriefs in Digital Spaces,
DOI: 10.1007/978-3-319-05098-0_4, © The Author(s) 2014

Table 4.1 Results of data analysis for the life cycle approach

Indicator	Required maturity level reached?
Dominant design: distributors	Cautiously yes; moved from dealer to service provider with heavy focus on IT-service; shift towards a 3PL model unlikely
Dominant design: 3PLs	Yes; two stable business models
Number of firms: distributors	National level: unclear; provincial level (Beijing): cautiously yes; three main players
Process versus product innovation: distributors	Cautiously yes; heavy investments in logistics centres and IT; however, IT services often have a product emphasis
Vertical linkages: manufacturer—distributor	No; arm's length relations dominate
Vertical linkages: distributor—hospital	Yes, clear signs of intensive vertical cooperation; extensive building of system-to-system links
Vertical linkages: 3PL—manufacturer/distributor	No; 3PLs are kept at arm's length; few indications of systems integration
Horizontal linkages: manufacturers	No; if horizontal cooperation exists (very rare) it is facilitated by third parties
Horizontal linkages: distributors	Cautiously yes as towards the end of the period of observation there are clear indications of indirect/assisted horizontal cooperation with a focus on B2B platforms
Horizontal linkages: 3PLs	No indications of horizontal collaboration
Application portfolio: manufacturers	No; while manufacturers have internally integrated systems, few have begun to integrate across company boundaries
Application portfolio: distributors	Yes for advanced firms; IT use varies significantly with most advanced firms having internally integrated systems (but not yet internally standardized product codes); towards the end of the period of observation, external systems integration with hospitals becomes wide-spread
Application portfolio: 3PLs	Yes for advanced firms; only large firms have internally integrated systems and offer Electronic Data Interchange (EDI) capabilities to their customers
Application portfolio: hospitals	Cautiously yes; over the period of observation, many hospitals have integrated their initially separate patient information and inventory systems; moreover, they also increasingly rely on system-to-system links with distributors

The maturity of IT use on the company level is operationalized through five indicators, derived from the Stages Hypothesis described above, of which we here only describe the indicator called 'application portfolio' since this was the only indicator for which we could collect sufficient data. The other indicators are: IT budget, IT resources, user awareness, and management control. These other indicators are only necessary for positioning a company's learning progression within one era (data processing, micro, network) while we are here only interested in whether companies have entered the network era.

The application portfolio should change in a characteristic way as companies move through the three eras described by the Stages Hypothesis. Specifically, the

Table 4.2 Results of our data analysis for the teleological approach

Intended effects regarding drug procurement	Establishment and expansion of centralized bidding systems based on e-commerce platforms; this intention is very consistent over the period of observation and across several government agencies
Intended effects regarding standardization	Establishment of unified drug names and barcoded numbers for smallest packing units; consistent over the last 6 years within SFDA
Intended effects regarding industry structure	Consolidation of the industry (distributors and manufacturers) and separation of drug sale and hospital operations; consistent over the last 6 years
Intended effects regarding drug prices	Unification and reduction of drug prices; recent efforts (since 2009) are in line with a consistent push towards lower prices over the last 14 years
Intended effects regarding IT use	Creation of Electronic Patient Records (EPR), but so far only on the level of individual hospitals
Unintended effects regarding standardization	Firms have learned to wait for government to set standards; however, fractions within government (between departments and levels) prevent successful standard setting by government
Unintended effects regarding industry structure	Because of regional organization of government, the main lever to consolidate the industry, increasing licensing requirements, often leads to regional fragmentation of the market
Unintended effects regarding industry practice	One intention of government in instituting the centralized e-bidding system was to be better able to monitor hospital purchasing behaviour; while that objective was not reached due to the use of non-standardized product codes, several unintended effects resulted, namely (1) increased susceptibility for corruption; (2) prevention of centralized procurement within hospital chains because of local bidding rules; (3) reduced potential for economies of scale because of local bidding rules
Unintended effects regarding IT use	The objective to establish electronic platforms for bidding and transacting has hampered efforts to integrate business processes and systems between distributors and hospitals; in contrast, increased regulatory requirements (aimed at consolidating the industry) have promoted such integration; also, local bidding rules prevent the establishment of a national bidding system

Table 4.3 Results of our data analysis regarding the institutional context

Institutional context: trade associations	Due to a legacy as former government agencies, industry associations lack the clout to coordinate the industry, including coordination through standardization
Institutional context: cultural factors	No clear indications of a direct influence of national culture

portfolio of applications should indicate that companies have integrated systems internally as well as externally.

Regarding the teleological approach, we have reconstructed government intentions through a content analysis of official documents such as guidelines, policies, 5-year plans, and laws, issued by various government agencies. Moreover, we have used a bottom-up coding method to identify unintended effects of government action.

Intended effects were classified into policies regarding:

- Drug procurement
- Drug prices
- Standardization
- Industry structure
- IT use

Unintended effects were classified into those regarding:

- Standardization
- Industry structure
- Industry practice
- IT use

Moreover, through our bottom-up coding processes two additional categories were created, namely 'institutional context' and 'national culture'.

Tables 4.1, 4.2 and 4.3 summarize the results of our data analysis. In the next chapter, we further synthesize these results into five high-level findings. Appendix I contains the detailed results of our data coding.

Chapter 5
Findings

We synthesize the results of our data analysis into five high-level findings.

I. *As the industry matures and as firms integrate systems internally, vertical linkages become more cooperative and include the establishment of system-to-system connections*

The evolution of the industry is most notable with regard to the role of distributors. While initially distributors essentially acted as dealers, buying drugs cheaply and selling them with a mark-up to hospitals or other distributors, those surviving multiple rounds of increasing regulatory requirements evolved to become service-providers for manufacturers and hospitals. Most notable among these changes is a push towards positioning themselves as comprehensive logistic players, helping hospitals to streamline their internal logistical processes, integrating information systems, often building these systems for hospitals, and connecting hospital information systems to their own enterprise systems. This is usually done through intermediate platforms, called B2B platforms in the industry, to which the systems of hospitals and distributors are connected. Initially, this process was not fully automated, involving the manual up- and downloading of business data. However, later on interfaces were built, again by the distributors, to connect the internal systems to these platforms to enable automatic processing of business data. We interpret this as evidence for our life cycle hypothesis in that a progression on both levels, the company and the industry level, towards maturity as defined by our multi-level framework, triggers more intense vertical collaboration which includes the building of system-to-system linkages. In these, initially bilateral, linkages we see the core of the emerging information infrastructure that is thus built based on evolving business models that emphasize services more than products and that, in turn, emerge as the industry matures and as companies have successfully mastered network era information technologies.

II. *As the industry matures and as firms integrate systems internally, firms engage indirectly in horizontal cooperation, facilitated by third parties*

K. Reimers et al., *Innovating in a Learning Community*, SpringerBriefs in Digital Spaces, DOI: 10.1007/978-3-319-05098-0_5, © The Author(s) 2014

Towards the end of the period of observation, we find clear indications of attempts to cooperate with competitors (horizontal cooperation) among distributors. The need for this cooperation arises from the increased reliance on the newly built B2B platforms. Typically, a hospital asks its main supplier, a distributor, to build such a system. Once in place, it then expects its other distributors to also use this platform which imposes an increasing burden of system maintenance on distributors. They now have to link to multiple, proprietary platforms used by their hospital customers and built by other distributors. Apart from having to built communication interfaces that connect their internal systems to these platforms, a major compatibility issue arises from the use of proprietary product codes. Almost every player in the industry uses their own product codes; however, since hospitals have a strong bargain position, they request that distributors map hospital codes onto their internal codes which increases the administrative burden related to incompatible systems. In this context, distributors have begun to build B2B platforms in such a way that it becomes easier for other distributors to connect to them. Some distributors even offer a product code mapping function which relieves other distributor users of the platforms to do that mapping internally. In some cases, distributors have attempted to jointly build B2B platforms but such cooperation was not yet successful. Also, direct cooperation among distributors only occurs if facilitated by a third party such as a hospital. Yet, the stance towards horizontal collaboration has significantly changed. While in the past B2B platforms were seen as strategic tools, they are now seen as potential areas of cooperation. The main rationale for such increased cooperation was the expectation of reciprocal behaviour. For example, a distributor who makes it easy for a competitor to connect to a B2B platform it has developed expects the same in cases that its competitor builds such a platform. One implication of this behaviour is that such collaboration only works among competitors of roughly equal size and market share.

III. *Government policies to establish an e-bidding platform have hampered the development of system-to-system links*

The establishment of third party e-commerce platforms to support the exchange of business data between hospitals and distributors is a very clear and enduring theme in government action. Yet, the measures taken to implement this objective actually hamper the efforts by firms to better integrate their information systems along the supply chain. First, third party e-commerce systems are used in parallel to privately developed B2B platforms so that both types of systems need to be maintained and operated. Second, repeated efforts by government to set up such systems have discouraged private efforts in this direction as firms have learnt to hold back from investment if they see government moving into the field. For example, one distributor has given up efforts to set up an open platform that could be used by hospitals as well as by distributors after government has started a similar initiative. Third, government lacks expertise in setting up and running such systems; as a result, they need to rely on the help of private firms for this purpose. This, in turn, creates artificial monopolies or opportunities for corruption which causes firms to adopt a very sceptical stance towards these platforms. Thus, we find that government action to directly build an information infrastructure may actually hamper the development of that infrastructure.

IV. *Government policies to consolidate the industry have helped to develop private B2B platforms and to marginalize the government mandated e-commerce platforms*

In contrast, government-driven policies towards faster and more pronounced industry consolidation have pushed the adoption of B2B platforms. This resulted from the increased focus on services and efficient supply chain management which, in turn, required an integrated information infrastructure across company boundaries. In contrast, companies are reluctant to integrate government-mandated e-commerce platforms into their business processes. On the one hand, there is a significant degree of scepticism towards these platforms, as described above; on the other hand, it is generally known that the main intention of government in building these systems is to better supervise the purchasing behaviour of hospitals and the sales practices of distributors. This reinforced the sceptical stance of companies and led to the marginalization of these systems.

V. *Government-driven standard-setting has prevented the industry from developing e-commerce standards*

As described above, a major hurdle towards building an information infrastructure is the lack of unified product codes. While all industry participants agree that standardization of product codes is necessary, they do not see any possibility of actually creating such a standard. The reason is that companies have learned to wait for government to set standards. This has worked in many areas but it turns out that the issue is so complex that government itself feels unable to go forward with mandating a standard product code. The reasons are the many fractions that exist between the several governmental agencies involved in supervising and regulating the industry as well as the inconsistent implementation of central government policies on lower governmental levels (provinces, municipalities). For example, standard product codes mandated by the State Food and Drug Administration (SFDA) are often not used or used only in parallel to proprietary codes. Moreover, the SFDA codes only cover a part of all prescription drugs and no Over The Counter medicines (OTCs). In addition, trade associations are seen as too weak to fulfil the function of a standard setter or facilitator. Actually, trade associations are often former government agencies which now have lost their clout over the industry. Also, it is beyond the mandate of these (state-controlled) organizations to collaborate among one another, which would be necessary since there are many associations in the industry.

Chapter 6
Theoretical Implications

We synthesize our findings into three hypotheses that provide a first set of intermediary conclusions.

I. *Development of an information infrastructure is a multi-level phenomenon*

Our data clearly reveal that an information infrastructure is gradually emerging over the period of observation. While in the first period (2004–2006) no any hints could be detected that speak of individual or collective efforts to align information systems so as to enable seamless information flow across multiple supply chain stages, companies engage in many and varied activities that are not only aimed at integrating information systems vertically, i.e. between customer and supplier, but also horizontally, i.e. between competitors, towards the end of that period. This change coincides with notable developments on both the organizational and the industry level. On the organizational level, companies have, often for the first time, built and integrated organization-wide information systems. Towards the end of our period of observation, firms across all supply chain stages (manufacturers, distributors, logistics firms, hospitals) posses integrated information systems to manage their core operational processes, in many cases derived from standard ERP software.

On the industry level, significant changes are observable as well. To begin with, the distribution industry is consolidating. However, this quantitative change coincides with significant qualitative changes. The business models of the several types of players become more clearly defined and standardized across the whole industry, vertical relationships between firms change from a distanced, price-oriented type towards more collaborative and integrated forms. Finally, horizontal relationships become manifest while, at the beginning of the period of observation, firms were often not even aware of who their competitors were. As competitive relations stabilized and intensified, firms also began to engage in collaborative actions with their competitors.

We believe that both these developments, integration of information systems on the organizational level and consolidation of relations among firms on the industry level, are crucial antecedents for an industry-wide information infrastructure. We

K. Reimers et al., *Innovating in a Learning Community*, SpringerBriefs in Digital Spaces, DOI: 10.1007/978-3-319-05098-0_6,

thus conclude that our life cycle approach is supported by our findings: the main determinant for the emergence of an industry-wide information infrastructure is the degree of maturity on both the organizational and the industry level.

II. *Development of an information infrastructure involves cooperation among competitors ('Coopetition') the concrete form of which is shaped by institutional factors*

The nature of cooperation among competitors was new and interesting to us. From a western perspective, one would expect firms to engage in explicit, carefully delimited joint projects carried out in formal settings such as standardization committees. However, actors in the Chinese pharmaceutical distribution industry were looking either to government or to important customers as catalysts for their cautious first steps towards collaboration with competitors. Moreover, the scope of these projects often were not delimited in advance but were allowed to evolve, sometimes creating precarious situations for competitors. The main mechanism to make this work is an expectation of reciprocity. A company that is willing to cooperate with its competitor on a specific project expects that such behaviour is reciprocated in situations were it depends upon the cooperation of its competitors. In contrast, collaboration among competitors in the West is typically based on a general common understanding of industry needs, acceptable and clearly defined areas of cooperation (vs. areas of competition) and an appeal to norms of fairness and reasonableness. We therefore believe that the form of cooperation among competitors is shaped by institutional and cultural factors while the need for such cooperation arises from the two-level life cycle described above. Institutional factors include government actions, the overall institutional structure of the industry, notably the nature and character of trade associations, and national culture. Among these three factors, we found governmental actions most strongly related to the type of systems that emerge. Moreover, governmental action was most consequential through unintended effects which speaks for the institutional character of this type of influence.

III. *Discourses on possible routes for collective action require dedicated 'places' that enable open discussion freed from competitive necessities*

Through creating the Learning Community we found that this was the only opportunity for open exchange among actors in the industry in general and competitors in particular. Occasions for cooperation arise outside the Learning Community but take place in settings that emphasise the competitive nature of relationships, e.g. when a hospital asks its distributors to jointly develop an ordering platform. While we cannot yet claim to have shown that our Learning Community has influenced the development processes associated with the emerging industry-wide information infrastructure, we clearly notice the need for a free exchange of ideas and experiences that actors have expressed in our workshops and that they admit could never have been voiced in the past. We also notice that our workshops have greatly improved the mutual understanding of industry players and are confident that such improved mutual understanding will eventually facilitate more intensive collaborative relationships among industry players. However, we also notice the strong influence of government action in all respects. For example, firms so far do not show any willingness to jointly engage in standardizing product codes for medicines, a crucial step towards the development of an open industry-wide information infrastructure. Rather, they wait for government to provide such standards. Government agencies, on the other hand, seem hesitant to come forward with such proposals as they may be openly or factually rejected by industry.

We therefore believe that, whether a place for open dialogue will actually influence the development of the industry information infrastructure will, again, depend upon its institutional embedding. This may require that government representatives are involved in the Learning Community as well.

Chapter 7
Extensions

One interesting aspect of the emerging industry-wide information infrastructure not yet explicitly addressed is that two systems exist in parallel to one another, the government-imposed centralized e-bidding platform and the company-driven B2B platforms. While the government-imposed platform experienced, to some extent, a reduction in importance it continues to be used and we predict that it will persist for the next couple of years. This gives rise to the question of why, when both companies individually and industry collectively had reached the required maturity stage that our framework predicts is a precondition for the emergence of an industry-wide information infrastructure, companies did not extend the already existing centralized bidding platform that government required companies to use? As companies previously had not yet acquired the necessary IT skills to integrate this platform into their own systems which, moreover, where not yet internally integrated, they could have used the existing platform when they were ready for such integration. Similarly, a shift towards more cooperative horizontal as well as vertical relationships in the industry would have favoured joint efforts to evolve the existing platform towards an open information infrastructure. Instead, companies invested in a parallel infrastructure and also took on themselves the burden of maintaining both systems simultaneously. To answer this question, we draw on the findings of a second study that we conducted subsequently to the first study based on our multi-level life cycle-framework.

That second study uses another framework based on the network relations model by Schultze and Orlikowski (2004) and boundary spanning theory (Levina and Vaast 2005). Both these models have been used in the context of inter-organisational information systems and both draw on a common theoretical basis, namely Practice Theory. The framework distinguishes between two dimensions: inter-firm information systems integration and inter-firm network relations. Both dimensions are operationalized as a dichotomy. Inter-firm information systems integration can be existent or not, meaning that firms use some form of electronic link to exchange business data, in our case this only concerns electronic ordering so that this dimension can take on two values: e-ordering and no-e-ordering. Inter-firm network relations can be either socially embedded or arm's length. 'Socially embedded' means that actors use social relationships, characterized by

DOI: 10.1007/978-3-319-05098-0_7, © The Author(s) 2014

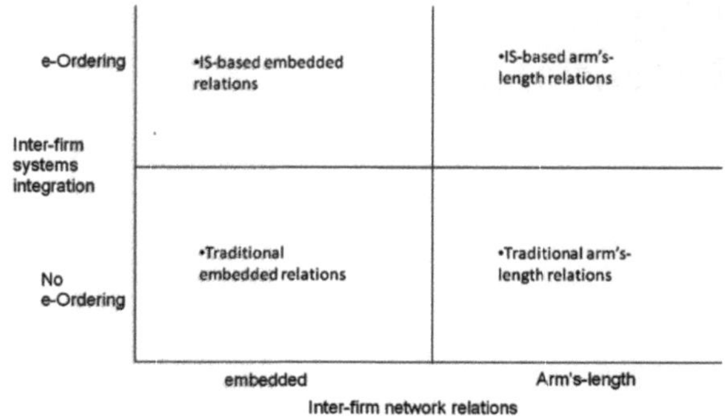

Fig. 7.1 Taxonomic framework for inter-firm network practices

expectations of reciprocity and identity, as a conduit for conducting business. In contrast, an arm's length relation is characterized by companies considering each other as substitutable business partners, treating price and quality as sole criteria for buying and selling decisions. Figure 7.1 visualizes the framework.

Drawing on the same material as described above, we have traced the development of the e-ordering systems over the period of observation. The results show that the development process can be effectively explained as a succession of three conceptual types of inter-firm practices described by our framework. E-ordering systems started in the first stage as a traditional socially embedded relation practice. In the second stage, the government attempted to shape an IS-based arm's length relations practice with the implementation of the centralized bidding and order processing platform. However, the practice did not evolve in the desired direction and the envisioned arm's length relations were not extensively established. On the contrary, the practice evolved to retain the socially embedded relations. The emergence of fragmented e-ordering systems reinforced these relations and the third stage can therefore be characterized as an IS-based embedded relations practice.

As discussed above, China has a huge, fragmented, and complicated pharmaceutical supply chain which came into being during the first stage from the 1980s to the early 2000s. It is estimated that there are 16 thousand drug distributors across the country, most of which are small ones. All the distributors keep trying to set up and maintain business connections with as many hospitals as possible. In the original no-e-ordering stage, such connections heavily depended on inter-personal relationships. The connections between distributors and hospitals were relatively stable and they all implicitly accepted that the business interactions would recur in the future. Based on such common assumptions and expectations, agents from distributors and hospitals would frequently conduct joint activities and engage in mutually dependent collaborations. Such a practice reflects the characteristics of traditional socially embedded relations.

Since such a vast and complex relational network was opaque and resistant to supervision, there were more and more "grey areas" that the government could not regulate. It was believed that this was the root cause of most of the corruption in the domain. In the second stage, the government initiated its efforts to shape the envisioned IS-based arm's length relations practice. According to this design and plan, if the centralized e-commerce platform had been successfully promoted and used all transactions would have migrated to it. Ideally, inter-personal relationships between distributors and hospitals would no longer be needed. Furthermore, the embedded relations would then be removed along with the "grey areas".

However, the practice did not evolve in the direction the government had intended. Instead, although the importance of e-ordering systems continued to grow, the practice demonstrated its resilience and turned out to retain socially embedded relations. It appears that there might be two major forces that drove the evolution away from the path towards arm's length relations.

The first force is that boundary spanners would try to preserve the social capital that they had accumulated in the practice. As pointed out in previous research, when an inter-organizational information system is implemented, it often requires boundary spanners to use their social capital for promoting the use of the system (Schultze and Orlikowski 2004). On the other hand, if the system were successfully used and the practice became arm's length, the original boundary spanners would lose their position in the relationship and their social capital would have been exhausted. Consequently, the boundary spanners-in-practice would continue to resist the evolution towards arm's length relations, and such resistance could be strong because of the spanners' power in the practice.

The second force that drove the evolution away from arm's length relations is the need for customized services. As some early research has suggested, in the long term, network technologies may facilitate the move towards personalized market arrangements (Malone et al. 1987). In the case of China, the centralized e-commerce platform deployed by government was not able to support such customized service requirements. Instead, since the first design goals were monitoring and supervision, the functional scope of the platform was limited.

Largely because of these two forces, the evolution of the e-ordering systems practice departed from the expected arm's length relations and moved into the third stage as an IS-based socially embedded relations practice.

References

Levina, N., & Vaast, E. (2005). The emergence of boundary spanning competence in practice: Implications for implementation and use of information systems. *MIS Quarterly, 29*(2), 335–363.

Malone, T. W., Yates, J., & Benjamin, R. I. (1987). Electronic markets and electronic hierarchies. *Communications of the ACM, 30*(6), 484–497.

Schultze, U., & Orlikowski, W. J. (2004). A practice perspective on technology-mediated network relations: The use of internet-based self-serve technologies. *Information Systems Research, 15*(1), 87–106.

Chapter 8
Answering the Research Question

Based on the findings of the two studies reported above, we now attempt to answer our overall research question and its sub-questions.

How do firms jointly develop open information infrastructures?

We observed three mechanisms that potentially account for the joint building of open information infrastructures. The first involves socially embedded relations among firms related in a supply chain relationship. The existence of these relationships, in the literature frequently discussed under their Chinese name 'Guanxi', greatly facilitated the building of electronic links between distributors and hospitals. In contrast to the government-imposed centralized bidding system, the B2B platforms built by distributors for hospitals were deeply integrated with internal information systems thus providing a first crucial element of the nascent information infrastructure. A next important element, the opening up of these systems for competitors, came about through two mechanisms: third party facilitation and expectations of reciprocal behaviour. Cooperation on building B2B platforms was supported and sometimes required by hospitals. There was also an indirect form of cooperation noticeable. Distributors made it easier for competitors to connect to B2B platforms by, for example, including a code mapping function that allowed for the translation of proprietary hospital product codes into the codes used by distributors internally. This behaviour was based on an expectation of reciprocity since distributors realized that they would also have to connect to systems built by their competitors. While there are probably many more mechanisms, some of which may be specific to particular institutional environments, we conclude that it is possible to build open information infrastructures based on self-interested behaviour of firms in an industry. However, for this to happen, specific conditions must prevail which cannot be taken for granted.

What motivates firms to engage in open innovation projects?

These conditions are to be found on the industry level. At the beginning of the period of observation there was a complete absence of joint engagement in the building of open information infrastructures, both in supply chain as well as in competitive relations. Only as the industry consolidated did these conditions

K. Reimers et al., *Innovating in a Learning Community*, SpringerBriefs in Digital Spaces, DOI: 10.1007/978-3-319-05098-0_8, © The Author(s) 2014

change to favour such joint effort. On the one hand, industry consolidation changed the nature of supply chain and competitive relations. Supply chain relations became more stable and long-term. Likewise, as competitive relations became less desperate, companies began to consider the possibility of collaborating in some aspects of their business activity. Specifically, the B2B platforms were no longer considered to be a battlefield of competition but became a necessity of doing business in the industry. This change coincided with a change in dominant business models. While distributors initially acted mostly as dealers, they later changed to become service providers offering a range of consulting and IT development services. This included the streamlining of internal processes and the building of information systems for which the B2B platforms were a required input rather than the main output.

How do firms delimit areas of proprietary innovation in open innovation projects?

In contrast to our expectations, companies did not attempt to clearly separate areas of proprietary innovation from areas suitable for open innovation. Rather, there was a fluid transition from one area to the other as companies changed their view on the nature of competition in the industry. The B2B platforms built by distributors were given to hospitals as a 'gift', along with control over these platforms. It seems that companies did not rely on proprietary innovations to build a competitive advantage. Instead, they considered continuous innovation to be the basis for their competitive success.

How do firms coordinate (initiate, negotiate, implement) the development of innovative infrastructures?

As discussed above, third party facilitation, socially embedded relations, and an expectation of reciprocity proved essential for coordination of joint activities. The development process was usually initiated by third parties, mostly hospitals. Hospitals also assisted in the further coordination process by holding joint meetings with distributors. Implementation was eased by social relations and an expectation of reciprocity.

How do processes and practices within firms enable and constrain such collective efforts?

The main constraint was the stage of company-wide learning with regard to absorbing new information technologies. Only if companies had developed a basic understanding of network era technologies were they able to participate in the development of an industry-wide information infrastructure. In contrast, when government imposed the centralized bidding system on the industry, most companies were not yet prepared for external systems integration. Accordingly, these systems were used as stand-alone platforms which required manual data input and extraction.

Do collective infrastructure projects give rise to specific industry-level practices that have their own rules, norms and ideational structures?

Apart form our own efforts in the form of setting up our Learning Community, we did not observe other manifest indications of an emerging industry-level practice. However, within the Learning Community, a sense of joint enterprise was clearly noticeable. All participants recognized the need for improvement and shared their concerns about the most pressing problems of the industry. A true interest in improving the 'health' of the industry was present, as was the willingness to share ideas and interpretations. Yet, the Chinese institutional environment does not support such activities. For example, trade associations do not command a lot of trust and are viewed with suspicion. Government is often afraid of talking directly to industry and the companies themselves have not yet begun to set up forums for joint activity and discussions.

If so, how do such emergent practices, in turn, constrain and enable activities by individual firms?

As these practices are nearly absent, except to the extent manifest in the Learning Community, we could not yet study how these practices might eventually impact on the practices in the individual firms.

Chapter 9
Managerial Implications

9.1 Towards the 2020 Enterprise

Partly based on our findings, but also extrapolating our own ideas, we suggest that the 2020 Enterprise has the following three characteristics.

(1) It has mastered network era technologies to perfection. It can easily and effortlessly connect with its business partners' information systems. Lack of standards does not pose an insurmountable obstacle while it has mastered all standards to be found in the industry. It has developed routine processes for connecting its internal systems with those of new business partners. It also understands the need for balancing costs and benefits of such links which may be distributed asymmetrically between the business partners. It looks beyond its adjacent supply chain stages to see the whole supply chain from final product to raw materials and how it can be integrated from an information perspective. It evaluates investments in supply chain integration from the perspective of market responsiveness rather than from a cost perspective.

(2) It is able to easily cooperate externally, including cooperation with its competitors. It understands the business and legal implications of such cooperation. It has developed clear guidelines regarding which projects it will support and how. It has set up dedicated organizational units that facilitate such cooperation. It is active in relevant forums such as standardization committees and has developed the technical expertise to competently participate in them.

(3) It leads the industry through cultivating industry-level practices. While it does not have formal authority over other companies in the industry, it has acquired a position which ensures that it is respected and listened to. It does this by establishing norms and rationales for joint industry-level action. It leads the industry by imbuing it with values of how work is to be conducted jointly and what constitutes fair competition. It organizes regular industry-wide meetings and also facilitates such cooperation through other means such as newsletters and white papers.

K. Reimers et al., *Innovating in a Learning Community*, SpringerBriefs in Digital Spaces,
DOI: 10.1007/978-3-319-05098-0_9,

9.2 Recommendations

Based on our findings, we would like to alert management to two issues. First, in emerging industries, information infrastructures may develop rapidly. Viewed from outside, it may appear as if they emerged 'out of the blue'. In our case, The emerging information infrastructure was hard to see or predict just 3 years ago. Thus, international companies, as opposed to domestic companies, are advised to look out for indications of emerging information infrastructures and then seek opportunities to actively engage in this process. In this way, they can demonstrate their willingness to contribute to the development of the whole industry and, at the same time, create the basis on which they might acquire legitimate industry leadership.

Second, we observed that existing industry practices may turn out to be much more resilient than is often assumed. That resilience is usually related to the history of existing practices which needs to be understood before they can be changed in desired directions. Even then, success is not guaranteed and change may resemble an evolutionary process rather than a designed change process. Thus, we recommend that, in trying to lead the development, companies abstain from trying to impose seemingly well designed processes on existing practices but rather create a forum in which these practices can be reflected upon and thus opened up for the possibility of change. As change initiatives are implemented, it will be necessary to continuously reflect on the contingencies of the ongoing change process and allow for deviations and adaptations at any moment. The skills required for this resemble those of the jazz musician more than those of the classically trained orchestra musician.

Chapter 10
Limitations

There are three possible limitations to our study and its results. The first two concern the domain that we studied. It might be the case that our findings are specific to both the Chinese context and the pharmaceutical distribution industry. Specifically the first limitation related to China as a research site may seem to suggest a high degree of specificity of our findings. There is a large literature which discusses the influence of Chinese national culture on adoption, implementation, and use of information technology. Thus, our findings may be limited to the Chinese context. However, based on the personal experience of one of the authors of this research study, who, as a foreigner, has lived in China for 5 years, we propose that most assertions about Chinese national culture have not survived China's rapid institutional change. What may have had a high degree of face validity just a few years ago has come to be viewed as an ancient practice as China is modernizing in all areas of social and economic life. We also note that one scholar who has followed the transformation of China, specifically from an IS perspective, suggests that phenomena such as Guanxi are not related to Chinese national culture but to a lack of a stable regulatory environment (Martinsons 2008). Moreover, that situation is changing rapidly too as China is increasingly subscribing to a rule-based way to govern its economy (Clarke et al. 2006). Therefore, we suggest that our findings might be applicable outside China too.

Second, our findings may be particular to the pharmaceutical distribution industry. The pharmaceutical distribution industry is special in that it is one of the most highly regulated industries for obvious reasons. This also results in a largely domestic character of the industry with few international players. (This was actually the reason that we had chosen this industry for our research as it seemed insulated from the forces of global competition and thus recommended itself for an international comparative study.) However, we note that the issues that came to the fore in our study as well as the responses by companies in the form of increased inter-company collaboration and the building of specific information systems are no different from what is known about other industries. Specifically, companies built standard ERP systems and connected these through electronic linkages known as Electronic Data Interchange that is known for three decades to have evolved in sundry industries (Swatman and Swatman 1992). Moreover, the supply

K. Reimers et al., *Innovating in a Learning Community*, SpringerBriefs in Digital Spaces,
DOI: 10.1007/978-3-319-05098-0_10, © The Author(s) 2014

chain management issues that were at the foreground of companies' concerns and activities are familiar from other industries as well (Lee et al. 1997). We therefore submit that our findings can potentially be generalized to other industries.

Finally, we have relied mostly on interviews for data collection, some of which, especially the earlier ones, could not be tape recorded because of a lack of trust by interviewees. As we became more familiar with the industry and as interviewees developed significant trust in us, we were later able to consistently tape record all our interviews though. However, to increase the validity of our findings, we have presented the core findings reported in this paper on the fifth LC workshop which took place on November 22, 2012, in Beijing. All results have been confirmed by the participating industry members and a government official.

References

Clarke, D. C., Murrell, P., & Whiting, S. H. (2006). The Role of Law in China's Economic Development, GWU Law School Public Law Research Paper No. 187, January 27, 2006.

Lee, H. L., Padmanabhan, V., & Whang, S. (1997). The bullwhip effect in supply chains. *Sloan Management Review, 38*(3), 93–102.

Martinsons, M. G. (2008). Relationship-based e-commerce: Theory and evidence from China. *Information Systems Journal, 18*, 331–356.

Swatman, P. M. C., & Swatman, P. A. (1992). EDI system integration: A definition and literature survey. *The Information Society, 8*, 169–205.

Appendix I
Data Synthesis

Introduction

In this appendix, we provide an intermediate step of our data analysis. Specifically, we summarize the results of our data coding in a way that allows all claims made here to be traced back to our data codes but allows these claims to be seen coherently so that a first evaluation of the findings is facilitated. Numbers in square brackets are references to our codes which, in turn, contain references to statements in our original data (both are not included in this appendix).

The text is structured according to the theoretical categories described above. In cases where the text for each category is long and complex, we also provide an evaluative summary (this is the case for most indicators). These are then the basis for our high level summary of the data analysis presented in tabular form above.

Dominant Design

Manufacturers

Too few codes and too varied types of manufacturers (from one product-company to firms with a broad range of products [a3, a4]) to make any claims about dominant designs.

Distributors

The business model of distributors has changed significantly over the period of observation. Initially (in the first period, 2004–2006), distributors acted mostly as dealers, buying and selling drugs. They bought drugs from manufacturers but also from other wholesalers [a5, a6]. As a consequence, obtaining price information was seen as a core competence [a8].

In the second period (2007–2009), distributors began to emphasise the logistical aspect more, partly by setting up dedicated units offering fee-based logistics services as the efficiency-aspect of distribution became more prominent [b1, b5, c5].

K. Reimers et al., *Innovating in a Learning Community*, SpringerBriefs in Digital Spaces, DOI: 10.1007/978-3-319-05098-0, © The Author(s) 2014

One reason is that government began to consider the possibility of separating pharmacy from hospital operations and of imposing a 'zero-margin' rule which would prevent hospitals from making money through drug sales [b7, b8]. This implies that prices become more transparent and thus proprietary price information less useful. However, it is also argued that distributors serve another important role, namely funding hospitals, since they have access to banks while hospitals don't [b3, b4, c4]. This is seen as preventing pure 3PLs from displacing distributors as dominant intermediaries [b2]. Related to the multi-tiered distribution system, ability to 'trace forward' (letting suppliers know who the final buyer of their products is) becomes an important part of the dominant business model [b6].

In the last period (2010–2012), distributors increasingly differentiate themselves by offering consulting and IT services [c7, c10, c11]. These include the building of B2B platforms for hospitals [c12] while, initially, distributors only offered tracing and tracking services to hospitals by giving them partial access to their internal systems [a3]. It is also said that online pharmacies strengthen the 3PL model versus the traditional distribution model [c1]. A hospital argues that distributors should not act as dealers, but rather as pure 3PLs, because they cannot effectively negotiate with manufacturers in case of quality problems [c8].

Vertical integration tendencies are observable over the whole period, initially only backward integration [a1, a4, c9], later on also into distribution (retailing) [c3, c9]. Distributors even start to operate warehouses in hospitals [c14] while this might remain a niche for some time [c13].

Contrary to some claims [a1], so far no distributor has reached a national scale of operations [a7, c2]. However, the industry leader (Guo Yao) is on its way to offer nation-wide services [c6].

Summary: The business model is evolving rapidly; initially, distributors essentially act as dealers, towards the end they become service providers, emphasizing IT-based services; these include systems integration for better logistical management; logistics services are also emphasized more but it does not seem likely that distributors will switch towards a pure 3PL model. The major distributors are rather similar in their service-approach so that it is justified to speak of a dominant design in their business model.

Third Party Logistics Providers (3PLs)

The development of this industry is tightly linked to that of the distribution sector. The data are not sufficient to document possible large-scale change over the period of observation.

The logistics industry is relatively new (about 10 years old) [b8, b12, b14] but, in contrast to the distribution industry, has some players that offer national coverage [b2, b6, b7, c2] while most participants are small firms with simple and local operations and with value-added services limited to re-packaging [b11]. Traditional logistics firms increasingly set up dedicated pharmalogistic units [b2, b4, b5].

Advanced firms offer differentiated services including warehouse management [b1], importation [b7], and complete ordering and fulfilment services [b3] while mostly firms compete on service level and price [b9]. In contrast to the distribution industry, customers are generally manufacturers rather than hospitals [b7].

As mentioned above (see 'Distributors'), the industry is rather sceptical regarding the possibility to replace distributors as dominant intermediaries [b10, b13] while the rise of online pharmacies may be the crucial lever for such a change [c1].

Summary: There are actually two business model of 3PLs: small, locally operating firms mostly offering transportation and simple warehousing services; large, national players offering advanced services based on sophisticated IT-systems. Both models seem to be stable; while it is said that the industry is young, that only refers to the second business model; the players here are mostly established international firms that imported their business models.

Hospitals

Data too limited to make broad claims. However, one significant change concerns the possible separation of pharmacy from hospital operations. Some hospitals have begun to outsource warehouse operations as a response to that trend [c1, c2] but it is not clear whether this model can be adopted by the industry at large [c3, c4].

EC intermediaries (third parties)

Only three codes. The business model has been created and imposed by government [context information]. Industry participants do not see any operational benefits offered by these firms [b1] so that it is unlikely that they will survive if government mandates ends. Haihong as the largest (and only remaining) EC intermediary in Beijing charges a combination of fixed and transaction fees to distributors rather than hospitals [c1]. In addition, every extra service like building interfaces is charged separately [c2].

No. of Firms, Firm Size

Manufacturers

No sufficient information to makes general statements.

Distributors

It is generally hard to obtain reliable data. Industry participants may also rely on outdated or wrong figures. However, it seems that the number of distributors actually fluctuates while there is no general trend over the period of observation. For example, the number of 17,000 distributors is mentioned at the beginning as well as at the end of our period of observation [a2, c6]. On average (over the period of observation), the number of firms mentioned is roughly 6000 [a1: 8000; a2: 5000, a5: 3000–4000, b3: 10,000, b6: 6000, c1: 4000–5000].

While sometimes statements by industry participants suggest that the number of wholesalers is declining, partly as a result of government intervention [a5, b6, c1], it is also said that the number bounced back because local governments protect firms in their provinces [b3]. A claim that the number of distributors has dropped as a result of the bidding systems [a3, b1], however, seems to be credible as there are indications of strong concentration in Beijing at the end of the period of observation [c3, c4] while explicit government efforts to reduce the number of distributors in Beijing have failed [c2]. It is expected that reducing the number of distributors will still take some time [b4, c5].

Summary: Focusing on the sheer number of firms does not allow for any clear conclusions, mostly because the numbers are not reliable but also because this number is highly political in that it is a target variable for government policy. However, on the provincial level (in Beijing) the industry seems to have consolidate with three main players dominating the market.

3PLs

Data insufficient.

Hospitals

No data.

Process Versus Product Innovation

Only 9 codes in total, 6 for distributors, 2 for 3PLs, and 1 for manufacturers. Only those for distributors will be interpreted.

Beginning in the second period (2007–2009) there are indications for a strong focus on process innovations among distributors [c3]. Investments are made in large logistics centres [b1] but IT is also increasingly seen as critical for the business [b2, c1] while third-party e-commerce systems did nothing to lower operational costs [b3]. B2B platforms built by distributors, however, have a strong product orientation as they are seen mainly as a means to win new business [c2].

Vertical Linkages

Manufacturer–distributor

Distribution carries two meanings: distributors act as logistical firms as well as sales agents for manufacturers. (Manufacturers have to sell through officially licensed distributors and thus cannot market drugs directly [a13].) Distributors' sales function seems to be relatively more important than their logistical function as sales targets are agreed [a5] and manufacturers use the promise of 'promoting' second-tier distributors to first-tier distributors as a main incentive [a7]. Manufacturers ensure that distributors do not also carry similar products by competitors [a4, a15]. This shows that the role of distributors is not limited to logistical tasks but also includes marketing and sales. (However, manufacturers also have own sales agents who visit hospitals [Manufacturer–hospital, a1, a3, a4].) By the same token, manufacturers hesitate to change their distributor (for a given drug) because they fear that that distributor may then lessen its efforts to also sell other products of that manufacturer that it might also carry [c2] while contracts are renegotiated on a yearly basis [a5]. Manufacturers use several to many distributors [a6, a14, b6] but maximally three for a given product [c3] while distributors similarly carry the products of many manufacturers [a2] but, as mentioned, such that competitive conflict is avoided.

Apart from their ability to effectively market drugs, distributors are also evaluated on whether they pay quickly [a14] while distributors, in turn, demand shorter delivery cycles [a3, a12].

Regarding electronic links, the situation varies. Some manufacturers and distributors have built EDI links [a1, a9] while others solely rely on fax and telephone [a16, b2, b6]. However, no standards exist for EDI so that in cases in which EDI links are built extensive code mapping [a10, b3, b4] and bilateral specification of EDI interfaces is necessary [a11]. An interesting kind of application is a forward tracing system that manufacturers build in order to know where their products finally end up [a8]. This is difficult to know since distributors often sell to other distributors rather than to hospitals directly [a6, b5]. In the last phase observed here, one distributor offers such a forward-tracing system to its supplier as a new service [c1]. This is the only sign of change in relationships over the period of observation.

Summary: Few signs of increased vertical cooperation; mostly, competitive pressure is used towards maximizing sales through a distributors. Few electronic links are built.

Distributor–hospital

The evolution of the relationship between distributors and hospitals shows both signs of continuity and dramatic change. The bargaining power of hospitals continues to be strong as there are signs of strong bargaining power in the first period [a4] as well as in the last period [c24, c31]. However, relations have become much more integrated and cooperative over the period of observation. To begin with, the number of distributors that a hospital uses is declining. At the beginning, hospitals used up to 30 distributors [a2] whereas at the end some hospitals have handed over warehouse management to just one distributor or are in the planning stages for such an arrangement [c12, c13, c21]. However, in these cases a hospital may still order from several distributors because no distributor carries the whole range of drugs needed by a hospital [context information]. In the last period (2010–2012), hospitals also expressly aim at reducing the number of distributors [c27] and prefer to work only with large distributors [c16]. Moreover, the ongoing change in relations is explicitly acknowledged [c14]. The key change in relations is a move to much more intense and close collaboration [c6] as evidenced by efforts to integrate information systems across distributors and hospitals—through so-called B2B platforms—[c19, c26, c28, c30, c35, c36], various forms of consultation and support regarding logistical processes and IT management [c2, c7, c8, c9, c10, c11, c15, c20, c29, c31, c41], and advanced forms of outsourcing and joint management, as already mentioned [c12, c13, c21, c39]. As a result, contracts also tend to become more long-term [c40].

Building electronic links generally requires the bilateral negotiation of interfaces and the mapping of product codes, with hospitals typically dictating the requirements [c1, c4, c18, c19, c23, c25, c28, c32, c34, c37] while there are some signs that platforms become more open so that distributors that have not built a particular platform can link to it more easily [c5, c30, c42]. Thus, while in the first two periods (2004–2006 and 2007–2009) data exchange occurred through third-party e-commerce platforms and was non-integrated and semi-automatic [a1, a3, b1, b2, b3, b4, b8, b9] with some hints at more advanced IT integration in the second period [b7], the third period saw a significant change in terms of increased degrees of inter-organizational information system integration.

Building these closer links is not free from conflict as distributors usually maintain close personal links into a hospital to support their ambitions which tends to create conflicting fractions in a hospital [c22]. Also, the B2B platforms built by distributors are aimed at maintaining personal relations rather than at directly increasing sales volumes with a hospital [c29, c35, c36]. One reason why these platforms are not used as 'strategic weapons' (known from the early IS literature and based on some form of lock-in) is that, while they are built by distributors (who also pay for them) [c19, c31], they are controlled (and owned) by hospitals [c3, c28]. Instead, a distributor needs to demonstrate good performance which, however, is a safe method of maintaining a relationship as hospitals will switch distributors only in cases of outright performance failure [c33, c38].

Distributors are seen as having the potential to integrate supply chains (involving hospitals and suppliers) [c17].

The benefits of integrated IS extend beyond the automation of data entry processes as distributors can obtain better demand information through them [c26].

Summary: Clear signs of closer vertical cooperation, involving value-added logistical services as well as various consulting services. Extensive building of system-to-system links is also evident; third-party e-commerce systems are not abandoned by marginalized. Nature of electronic links different from Western-style strategic weapons; rather, such systems are seen as gifts underpinning social relations.

Manufacturer–hospital

No sufficient data to make claims about the nature of that relationship or its change over time.

3PL–manufacturer/distributor

Some manufacturers as well as some distributors outsource parts of their logistical operations to 3PLs [a1, b1, b2, b7, b12, b26, b28, b30] while hospitals also started to use own trucks to pick up drugs [b13] (it is not clear, however, whether this is a general trend; it is also contrary to efforts by hospitals to outsource logistical operations to distributors, see 'distributor–hospital' relations). Relations are based on trust and an expectation of long-term continuity [b8, b15, b20]. So far, relations are not considered to be strategic, and thus non-exclusive, with price and performance of 3PLs being the main evaluation criteria [b8, b16, b20, b21]. However, one 3PL indicates that they aim at building a more strategic partnership with a customer [b17]. Some signs of deeper collaboration are noticeable such as joint planning, which is common [b8, b15, b22], and establishment of EDI links, which is much rarer [b4, b5, b10, b11], while many customers explicitly do not want to establish EDI links [b18]. Generally, there are few indications of IS integration between 3PLs and their customers; the norm is that 3PLs offer some visibility into their systems for tracking and tracing [b3, b6, b18, b27] while customers rather call in to inquire about shipments because such information is often not up to date [b3, b18] or receive status reports through email [b24].

The data are not sufficient to establish whether there is change or continuity over the period of observation; specifically, there is a scarcity of data for the first and the last period.

Summary: Vertical relations are kept at arm's length; while some EDI links are being built, many customers explicitly reject establishment of such links.

EC intermediaries–industry

Just three codes. EC intermediaries are third parties (either privately owned or government-owned) that operate B2B platforms. This is in contrast to distributors who operate such platforms as supply chain members and not as third parties (see 'Distributor–hospital' relationship).

Hospital groups have a fixed relationship with EC intermediaries [b1]. All intermediaries in Beijing use different data standards so that the bidding centre needs to 'harmonize' them [b2]. Similarly, hospitals use different data standards (see 'distributor–hospital' relationship) so that the EC intermediaries also need to harmonize the data they receive from hospitals [b3]. However, it seems that such harmonization (by the bidding centre as well as by the EC intermediaries) is not done consistently [context information].

Horizontal Linkages

Manufacturers

The industry consists of many small companies that often produce similar products (drugs) [c1]. As a result, firms find it difficult to join forces with competitors for purposes such as standardization or counterfeiting [a2, c1]. If cooperation does take place it is typically facilitated through a third party [a3, b1]. While entry barriers are high [a4] domestic firms, often starting as very small ones [context information], have succeeded in dramatically increasing their market share [a1]. This seeming contradiction might be explained by the nature of entry barriers, namely good relationships with hospitals and local governments [context information]. The data are insufficient to establish whether any change as occurred over the period of observation.

Distributors

Like in the manufacturing industry, distribution is highly fragmented and competition fierce since products (drugs) are very similar [c5, c7]. At the same time, firms often rely on competitors when servicing areas in which they do not have own operations [a2, c2] and even sell to other distributors on a large scale [a1, a3]. However, these business exchanges only occur when firms are not direct competitors, either because they do not both operate in one geographical region or because they do not have access to the same manufacturer [context information]. As a result, cooperation between competitors in all other cases rarely happens and if it does it tends to be facilitated by third parties (including government) [a4, c9, c10, c16]. The industry is characterized as immature and unable to share information [b2, c3]. Entry barriers are high because distributors need to maintain good relationships with hospitals [b1] and, in addition, need good relationships with government to obtain funds and licenses [context information]. However, it is speculated that the bidding system might benefit new entrants as it favours firms with more efficient processes [b3].

However, towards the end of our period of observation major players initiated joint projects which, however, initially failed, or are considering such cooperation [c4, c6, c8]. In addition, an increased degree of indirect cooperation is noticeable as distributors start to use each other's B2B platforms [c1]. While there are some indications that these platforms are also used to increase competitors' costs [c14] the main evidence points towards a more friendly approach [c11, c12, c18, c19, c20, c21]. Some distributors even include a code mapping function to make it easier for competitors to connect to these platforms [c13, c17]. This change of increased willingness to (indirectly) cooperate is explicitly acknowledged [c21]. The mechanism of such indirect cooperation seems to be the threat of reciprocal retaliation since even the large distributors will also have to use their competitors' platforms when servicing some hospitals [c11, c15]. This is in line with a more general practice of reciprocity that comes to the fore in market sharing arrangements [context information].

Summary: While horizontal contacts are rare overall, towards the end of the period of observation clear indications of cautious horizontal cooperation are noticeable, albeit mostly indirect and/or facilitated by third parties. Such indirect/assisted horizontal cooperation focuses on the B2B ordering platforms.

3PLs (Logistics firms)

Interview data only available for the second period (2007–2009).

The industry is still young, consisting of newcomers [b1] and established distributors who begin to offer logistical services in addition to their traditional wholesaling business [b1, b7]. So far, no clear industry leader has emerged [b1] although some see CNMC (Guo Yao) as an industry leader [b3]. Information about competitors is collected through unsystematic observation at customers' premises or own research [b4, b8]. Competition is fierce since services are not differentiated so that firms are evaluated only on the basis of service levels in relation to prices [b5, b10]. Since most firms are small and regionally focused, they are often forced to collaborate in order to offer logistical services in an area in which they do not maintain own operations [b1, b2, b6]. Otherwise, firms do not collaborate or share information [b8, b9].

Summary: No indication of horizontal collaboration noticeable; most firms even don't know who their competitors are.

Hospitals

Only three codes from the last period (2010–2012).

Hospitals do not have sufficient motivation to jointly standardize product codes [c1] or use one another's product codes [c3] while some are considering the possibility of joint purchasing through a common B2B platform [c2].

Management Control, User Awareness, IT Budget

Practically no data in these categories.

IT Resources

Only three codes from manufacturers (not separately tabulated):

"Almost 10 % of total workforce in China committed to its main distribution system (001)"

"Has an internal team for mapping product codes of distributors to own system (003) as well as other types of code (incl. dates) (004); 3–4 people, 70,000 messages monthly (005)"

"Have a small in-house IT department (005)"

These are interesting in that manufacturers seem to spend significant resources on IT services that are related to the specific structure of the pharmaceutical distribution industry, namely a forward tracing system (related to the multi-tiered structure of the distribution industry) and a code mapping team (related to the lack of standards for product codes).

Application Portfolio

Manufacturers

Few codes. It is probably safe to say that manufacturers use ERP systems [a1, b1, b3, b4], have internally standardized product codes [b4], but do not yet have any significant degree of external systems integration (except for narcotics) [c1, c2] with probably foreign manufacturers being more advanced in this regard [context information].

Data not sufficient to make any claims about large-scale change over the period of observation.

Distributors

IT use of distributors varies significantly with many small firms still not using computers at all [b1, c8] and some firms, the larger ones, having built integrated ERP systems [b3]. However, even the largest and supposedly most IT-experienced firm (Guo Yao) still has not standardized product codes across regional divisions [b2, c6].

In the last period, some significant change is observable. While distributors initially (in the first period, 2004–2006) used third party platforms to download orders as a result of government mandate [c10] later on they had built simple B2B platforms that were used by hospitals and distributors to exchange business data, albeit often still not integrated into their respective internal systems [c1, c2, c3, c4, c7]. Yet, increasingly system-to-system links are being built [context information; see also 'Distributor–hospital vertical linkages' and 'Application portfolio, hospitals'] while before such platforms were used, order data were taken over the phone with hospitals using highly proprietary product codes that required significant experience on the side of distributors to be properly interpreted [c9].

3PLs

Few codes, only from large firms. Data insufficient to make claims about longitudinal changes.

The big players have internally integrated IS which are often internally developed rather than standard ERP systems [b1, b5, b6, b7, b8, c1] which is crucial for their operations [b2]. EDI data partly processes automatically [b3, b4].

Hospitals

While hospitals had inventory management and patient information systems at the beginning of our period of observation [a1], the last period (2010–2012) is characterized by a significant push towards internally and externally integrated systems. Partly depending upon the help of distributors, hospitals strived to integrate internal systems which mostly meant integrating ERP systems and HIS (hospital information systems) [c1, c6, c9, c10, c13, c14, c32]. For some hospitals, ERP systems became essential tools for operations management [c2] even though general IT management in hospital supposedly lags behind that of distributors [c4, c7, c15, c30]. In some cases, hospitals maintain separate systems in order to protect sensitive data [c17, c23]; in smaller hospitals, internal systems are still fragmented [c16, c25, c26, c28, c35].

Regarding external systems integration, hospitals initially used mandatory third-party platforms, use of which is still ongoing [context information, c37], but quickly came to rely on B2B platforms built by distributors [c5]. While, at the beginning of the last period (2010–2012) these were not yet integrated with internal IS [c8, c18], towards the end there are many hospitals that have successfully automated external business communication [c3, c21, c22, c24, c33].

Many hospitals have built e-prescription systems [c27, c31, c34]. Some hospitals have also externally integrated payment systems [c29].

Advanced applications (electronic drug cabinet) are planned [c36]. However, hospitals are struggling to trace drugs on the batch level because of non-standardized batch numbers [c9, c11, c12, c13, c15].

Government Action (Intended Effects)

Regarding centralized drug procurement

- Several national authorities issue legislation to encourage the expansion of centralized drug procurement [2] (2004)
- SFDA regulates the use of e-bidding/e-commerce systems (three actions, 2004, 2005, 2006) [3, 4, 5] (2004–2006)
- Various agencies (including central government) issue new rules for the drug bidding process [13] (2009)
- Central government issues new guidelines regarding the bidding process, including a rule that provinces are responsible for regulating the bidding process and drug distribution [16] (2010)
- Various agencies (including central government) rule that all state-owned non-profit hospitals above county level must procure drugs only through the bidding process [17] (2010)
- Several ministries issue the 12th Five-year plan for the pharmaceutical industry which concerns, among other issues, comprehensive implementation of centralized bidding system [29] (2012)

Summary: Establishment and expansion of centralized bidding systems based on e-commerce platforms; this intention is very consistent over the period of observation and across several government agencies.

Regarding standardization

- SFDA regulates (standardizes) drug names [6] (2006)
- SFDA rules that manufacturers need to print SFDA barcodes on smallest packaging unit and that manufacturers and distributors need to join an electronic supervision system (for tracking & tracing drugs throughout the supply chain) run by the SFDA [18] (2010)
- SFDA issue plan to further expand its supply chain supervision (tracking & tracing) system based on SFDA barcodes [30] (2012)

Summary: Establishment of unified drug names and barcoded numbers for smallest packing units; consistent over 6 years within SFDA.

Regarding industry structure

- SFDA separates wholesaling from retailing business [7] (2006)
- Central government requires re-registration of all drugs [8] (2006)
- SFDA breaks monopoly of Guo Yao in distribution of narcotic drugs [9] (2006)
- SFDA tightens regulatory requirements for distributors and manufacturers [10] (2007)
- Beijing authorities (health dept., SFDA) attempt to consolidate distributors but quickly gives up on this plan [14] (2009)
- Commerce ministry outlines a plan to consolidate the distribution industry and to strengthen independent retail pharmacies [22] (2011)
- SFDA tightens regulatory requirements for manufacturers and distributors [23, 24] (2011)
- Commerce Ministry pushes for further industry consolidation [28] (2011)
- Several ministries issue the 12th Five-year plan for the pharmaceutical industry which concerns, among other issues, separation of drug sales and hospital operations and the further consolidation of manufacturing and distribution industries [29] (2012)

Summary: consolidation of the industry (distributors and manufacturers) and separation of drug sale and hospital operations; consistent over 6 years.

Regarding pricing

- Another round of health care reform started by central government; zero mark-up policy mentioned; also created: a basic drug catalogue [11, 12] (2009)
- Beijing government rules that all secondary and higher level hospitals sell drugs at the same price [19] (2010)
- National Development and Reform Commission plans nation-wide uniform drug retail prices; selects 50 varieties as a pilot [21] (2011)
- National Development and Reform Commission investigates drug prices and issues regulation regarding price setting [26, 27] (2011)
- National Development and Reform Commission in total issues 30 calls for drug price reductions [31] (1998–2012)

Summary: Unification and reduction of drug prices; recent effort (since 2009) are in line with a consistent push towards lower prices over the last 14 years.

Government Influence (Unintended Effects)

Influence on standardization

The role of government in standardization is ambivalent. On the one hand, firms expect government to impose standards [b4, b5, c8, c9], on the other hand, internal conflict between government departments and levels (central vs. provincial government) prevents government from setting standards [c2, c3, c7] or leads to different departments issuing competing standards [c4]. Also, government is unable or unwilling to organize a bottom-up standardization process [b2]. So far, the SFDA has had the most influence by establishing so-called FDA-codes [b1]. However, these do not cover the whole range of drugs [b7] and are often not used [b3] or used in parallel with proprietary codes [b1]. In cases where government did set a product code standard (for batch numbers), this is criticized as not sufficiently thought through [b6, c1]. However, on the provincial level there is an instance of successful product code standardization [c5]. It is suggested that government may use financial incentives to encourage adoption of an common product standard [c6].

Summary: Firms have learnt to wait for government to set standards; however, fractions within government (between departments and levels) prevent successful standard setting by government

Influence on industry structure

Government has a crucial influence on industry structure [b6, c1, c8], mostly exercised through licensing requirements. Thus, special licenses are required for selling to hospitals [b8, b9, b15] which, so far, are only given to traditional distributor-wholesalers [a4] but not to 3PLs [b4] (online pharmacies not yet allowed [b14] either). Similarly, licenses are required for offering pharmalogistics services [b3, b5]. Government uses this lever to influence industry structure by varying the licensing requirements [c8, c9]. For example, licensing requirements for 3PLs have continuously been increased [b11, b12] which also increased entry barriers. While this measure is aimed to increase industry concentration, licenses are generally locally or regionally limited which increases fragmentation of industry [a3, b10] even though distributors are formally allowed to operate in several provinces [a1]. In addition, conflict between central and provincial governments leads to uneven and often locally protectionists licensing practices, further fragmenting the market [b2, b7, b13, c2, c3, c5, c11] while even central government cannot act coherently because of the large number of involved departments [a2, b1, c4].

Another lever for government is pricing policy. For example, it is expected that if government implements a zero-pricing policy, hospitals will outsource all logistics, including the management of their drug warehouse, to distributors [c6].

Whether measures taken by government have the intended effect, however, is often unclear. One reason is that government considers it too risky to consult with industry before issuing new regulations [c7]. As a result, it is increasingly doubted, towards the end of the period of observation, whether government policies directed towards consolidating the industry will be successful [c10].

Summary: Because of regional organization of government, the main lever to consolidate the industry, increasing licensing requirements, often leads to regional fragmentation of the market. Whether efforts by government to reduce the number of firms is doubted because of a reluctance to consult with industry before issuing new regulations. To lower drug prices, government intends to impose a zero margin rule which will cause some hospitals to outsource logistics (furthering the separation of hospital operations and drug distribution)

Influence on industry practice

Apart from industry structure, government has also a strong influence on industry practices. One central aim of introducing the e-bidding/e-commerce platform was to be able to better enforce rules regarding hospital purchasing behaviour [a1, b2, c5]. However, it is generally doubted whether government was powerful enough to enforce these rules. On the one hand, it is simply doubted whether government is powerful enough vis-à-vis the bargaining power of hospitals [b1, b3, b4, b6]. On the other hand, failure to standardize product codes made it impossible to use the e-bidding system to monitor hospital purchasing behaviour [b5]. Introduction of the bidding system may have even weakened government because of increased opportunities for corruption [b8, c4]. Generally, companies attempt to maintain close bilateral relations with government to further their business interests [b9, b10, b15].

At the same time, the existence of local licensing rules has a strong, albeit unintended impact on various aspects of industry practice. For example, local bidding rules prevent hospitals from integrating their purchasing functions nationally [c1, c3]. Moreover, economies of scale in manufacturing are reduced, sometimes leading to decisions by manufacturers to stop production of crucial drugs [c2].

Interestingly, government seems to play a role that is otherwise considered to be the strength of trade associations, namely offering various services to companies [b12].

Assessment varies regarding the ability to effectively supervise the industry. It seems that this ability strongly depends upon the particular industry sector, with logistics being much easier to supervise than hospitals and pharmaceutical manufacturers [b7, b11, b13, b14].

Summary: One intention of government in instituting the centralized e-bidding system was to be better able to monitor hospital purchasing behaviour; while that objective was not reached due to the use of non-standardized product codes, several unintended effects resulted, namely (1) increased susceptibility for corruption; (2) prevention of centralized procurement within hospital chains because of local bidding rules; (3) reduced potential for economies of scale because of local bidding rules.

Influence on IT use

Government has also a significant influence on IT use, both intended and unintended. The use of e-commerce for drug ordering by hospitals became mandatory in 2004 [a1]. Similarly, the SFDA has issues detailed rules for IT use by distributors as part of its licensing requirements [b1].

It is not clear whether prevention of a national bidding system is intended or not; in any case, this is the result of local bidding rules [c1]. Similarly, increasing enforcement of regulatory rules in pharmaceutical distribution seems to push the adoption of B2B platforms developed by distributors [c2] while the attempt by government to set up such a platform itself [c4] has hampered efforts by distributors to develop such platforms [c3]. Also, government seems to depend upon the help of distributors in this effort [c5]. Yet, government is not very successful in this effort as companies are sceptical with regard to platforms operated by profit-oriented firms which are simultaneously backed by government [c6]. In addition, regulating e-commerce platforms seems to prevent further inter-organisational integration of IS [c7].

Summary: the objective to establish electronic platforms for bidding and transacting has hampered efforts to integrate business processes and systems between distributors and hospitals; in contrast, increased regulatory requirements (aimed at consolidating the industry) have promoted such integration; also, local bidding rules prevent the establishment of national bidding system.

Institutional Context

Influence of industry associations

Industry associations in China are considered to be much weaker than in other countries and to play different roles [a1, b2, b6]. Specifically, it is believed that industry associations can neither help firms to establish standards [a1, c3] nor do they offer useful services to companies [b5]. Rather, it is hoped that they address criminal behaviour in the industry [b4]. However, associations are themselves accused of engaging in illegal behaviour [b1]. Otherwise, their role is mostly to organize discussion forums and lobbying [a1, b2]; the legitimacy of the latter, however, is controversial [b1]. However, there seems to be a deviant opinion in that associations may play a crucial role in standardization and industry consolidation [b7, c2].

This overall situation might be related to the origin of industry associations. They are mostly former government departments [context information, c1], often headed by former government officials who, however, are no longer considered to have any power [c4]. Crucially, it seems illegal and illegitimate for associations to cooperate among themselves [c5].

There is are many associations in the industry [b2] while none exists specifically for pharmalogistics [b3, b6].

Summary: Due to a legacy as former government agencies, industry associations lack the clout to coordinate the industry, including standardization.

Influence of culture

Practical no indication for a direct influence of culture, except one code, which, however, may reflect a stereotype ("it is difficult to set up IS in China because people are not used to following rules" [c1]). Thus, no clear indications of a direct influence of national culture was found.

Appendix II
Development of Electronic Patient Records and Drug Tracking Technologies in China

Introduction

Since some time, China is undertaking a significant healthcare reform which aims at providing affordable universal basic health care. The waste caused by overused drugs and repeated medical examinations is one of the major reasons for the heavy medical expenses characterizing the Chinese healthcare system. Hence, the implementation of EPR (Electronic Patient Records) promises to be a solution to avoid repeated medical examinations and adverse drug reactions. Aside from high medical costs, drug counterfeiting is receiving wide attention as a public health issue. Due to the fragmented structure of pharmaceutical distribution and a large number of pharmaceutical manufacturers and distributors, it is still very difficult to trace drugs from production to end users, which opens numerous possibilities for drug counterfeiting.

The purpose of this appendix is to capture and present the historical development of EPR (Electronic Patient Records) and drug tracking technologies in China. To better analyze the key factors that are likely to have the greatest influence on the current state and future trend, we divided the historical timeline constructed from our observations into three periods. In the first period, application of information technologies emerged as a novel issue in the Chinese healthcare industry, when there was almost no specific regulation regarding EPR and drug tracking. A series of policies were then released after a new round of healthcare reform in the second period. In the third period, the consequences of these policies were observable. This appendix is mainly presented in narrative form, and the historical timeline presented in tabular form in the last section serves to provide a summary and synopsis of this appendix.

Data sources for this appendix mainly came from Chinese government websites, news collected in our research blog (http://blog.sina.com.cn/u/1808556792), and the workshop transcripts of the Learning Community of the Chinese Pharmaceutical Supply Chain.[1] In addition, a small number of published articles is used and referenced accordingly.

---

[1] Our research team has established a Learning Community for Application of Novel Information Technologies in the Pharmaceutical Supply Chain in China; a workshop for discussing major topics in the Chinese healthcare industry is held every 6 months in Beijing, and drug tracking and tracing was one of the topics. A blog which collects the relevant events was created by the research team in order to keep track of the development of Chinese healthcare industry.

K. Reimers et al., *Innovating in a Learning Community*, SpringerBriefs in Digital Spaces, DOI: 10.1007/978-3-319-05098-0, © The Author(s) 2014

Background on EPR

Electronic patient records are an application environment composed of the clinical data repository, clinical decision support programs, controlled medical vocabulary, order entry programs (computerized provider/physician order entry or CPOE), pharmacy programs (if applicable) and clinical documentation applications, and are used by providers to document, monitor and manage healthcare.[2] Deviating from the accepted EPR concept, in which different healthcare providers are able to make entries in and retrieve data from a commonly shared EPR system, the official definition given in the "Basic Standards for Electronic Patient Records (for trial implementation)" that was issued by SFDA does not include this requirement.

The first goal of EPR implementation was to provide a comprehensive documentation for medical disputes, as the number of medical disputes and violent incidents between doctors and patients has dramatically increased in China. Mistakes would commonly occur when doctors' handwriting is not legible. However, the adoption of EPR systems also obtained a second, even more important role under the circumstances of the Chinese healthcare reform, which is to decrease medical expenses by reducing repeated medical examinations as well as excessive drug consumption. Moreover, the integrated EPR systems can also help patients receive medical reimbursement across different regions. This has yet to be realized because the insurance centers do not have access to patient records outside their region.

Background on Drug Tracking

Drug tracking involves a process of determining the current and past locations (and other information) of drugs.[3] It is an extremely challenging task for a country like China where there are thousands of pharmaceutical manufacturers and distributors, with more than 150,000 registered drugs and over one million medical institutes[4] of which more than 90 % belong to community level healthcare centers and below.[5] Drug tracking is also an essential issue in terms of drug security and safety, since the number of victims of counterfeit drugs and expired drugs is growing every year.

---

[2] Definition taken from HIMSS (Healthcare Information and Management Systems Society), 2006.

[3] Definition taken from Wikipedia.

[4] Medical institutes here include all hospitals, community health service centers, rural health service centers, center for disease control and hygiene inspection offices in China.

[5] Gaojun Teng, Minglin Li, Vincent Li 2012, The Digital Revolution in China: PACS and Networks, Report from 8th Annual MIIT Conference, Toronto.

Historical Overview Roadmap of Electronic Patient Records and Drug Tracking in China

Emergence of Information Technologies in the Chinese Healthcare Industry (1990–2008)

The Open Door Policy in the early 1980s helped global information technologies enter the Chinese market. Meanwhile, several advanced manufacturers already started to implement MRP systems (Material Requirements Planning), which is seen as the predecessor of the modern ERP (Enterprise Resource Planning) systems. Modern information technologies were first introduced and used by the Chinese healthcare industry during the early 1990s, when some large-scale pharmaceutical companies and hospitals started to apply information systems for internal management.[6]

To carve out a firm position in the informatized global economy, the Chinese government decided to strengthen ICT (Information Communication Technology).[7] Therefore, the Ministry of Health issued a development plan for national ICT in the healthcare sector from 2003 to 2010, in which the government committed to raise investments for the construction of information technologies in public hospitals. Furthermore, the plan also pointed out the essential role of data standardization during ICT development.

According to a report by the Ministry of Health, about 80 % of tertiary hospitals[8] had adopted HIS (Hospital Information Systems) by the end of 2008, and pharmaceutical companies showed an even speedier development in terms of information systems adoption during this period.

EPR (Electronic Patient Records)

An official of the Health Ministry raised the topic of EPR construction at the 6th Medical Informatics Conference in 1994. Hospitals were thereby encouraged to implement EPR systems for patient information management. Furthermore, it was hoped that there could be some pioneering hospitals to lead the trend. Although the government has seen the need and the trend of EPR application, there was no legislation explicitly made for EPR during this period. The only related, supporting policy was the Electronic Signature Law in 2005, which recognized the validity of

[6] Yuqing Zhou, Boying Liu, Qiang Zhou 2005, ERP and Business Management: Theory, Methodology and System, published by Tsinghua University.

[7] Yu Hong 2008, Distinctive Characteristic of China's Path of ICT Development, International Journal of Communication, pp. 456–471.

[8] According to a hospital's ability to provide medical care, medical education, and conduct medical research, public hospitals in China are classified into three levels, namely primary, secondary and tertiary hospitals. Tertiary hospitals possess the highest level of medical services as well as research.

electronic documents. From then on, patient information in the EPR system carried the same legal validity as a paper-based signature or seal.

Unlike the ambivalent position of government, EPR software providers were much more proactive. They tried various ways to develop EPR-related software to meet the demands of hospitals at different stages, and market competition drove EPR application further forward. The EPR development in China can be divided into three phases[9]:

- In the first phase (2000–2002), the handwritten patient record was simply replaced by a free text document and its functions were very limited. It was basically a word file attached to the hospital information system; no specific interface allowing for automated data exchange and processing was developed during this period.
- In the second phase (2003–2007), more requests were made for user interface standardization so that all relevant patient information could be better sorted and compared. To extend its functions and to make the electronic patient records more professional, software providers started to develop specific EPR software separately from the hospital information systems. Doctors had a better user interface, and it was easy for them to search for specific patient information. However, the EPR software at this time was not integrated with the hospital information system.
- In the third phase, which began in 2008, hospitals started to realize that this fragmented software architecture would even increase their coordination costs since various decisions are based on patient information (e.g. clinic wards, hospital pharmacies, doctors etc.). Maintaining separate databases actually increases the workload if the patient information is not integrated in the hospital information system. Under these circumstances, hospital information system providers decided to acquire or to merge with EPR developers. Since then EPR no longer existed as individual software but as an integrated part of the hospital information system.

Drug Tracking

At the beginning of this period, there were only several hundred pharmaceutical distributors operating in this industry, and this number has risen several dozen times within the last decade.[10] Drugs need to pass many tiers in the supply chain before they reach patients, which unnecessarily lengthens the path for tracking the drugs and complicates the procedures. It is possible for a manufacturer to track their drugs in the first and second tier of their distributors, but it is very difficult to go further.

A drug barcode functions like a personal ID which gives access to relevant drug information, provides unique drug identification, and it is machine-readable. Thus, the drug barcode is an essential issue when drug tracking is mentioned.

---

[9] Chunhua Xu 2010, Clinical Application of Electronic Patient Records in China.

[10] Medicine Economic News 2010-10-27, p. 15.

Beginning in late 1990s, more and more pharmaceutical companies decided to adopt ERP (Enterprise Resource Planning) systems for their internal management. Naturally, development of internal product barcodes would be their next step. However, problems occurred when companies all had different drug barcode specifications, and those barcodes could not be automatically translated by the system. As a result, drug tracking through product barcodes was quite limited during this period; only a small group of advanced pharmaceutical distributors could track their own products in the system while most of the drug tracking process was actually paper-based. It was difficult to accomplish drug tracking throughout the whole supply chain.

Despite all the challenges mentioned above, there were some achievements in terms of drug tracking over this period. The only narcotics distributor in China, Sinopharm,[11] established a national network for the narcotics supply chain in 2001, in which all narcotic records were assembled. Therefore, it was possible to have a paper-based system for narcotics tracking at a national scale.

In addition, drug tracking also came up in the GMP (Good Manufacturing Practice) and GSP (Good Sales Practice) standards issued by SFDA (State Food and Drug Administration),[12] and in the modified version of "Measures for the Administration of Commodity Barcode", which can also apply to medicines. This offered an opportunity for a nationally standardized commodity barcode. However, the measures were not obligatory and only recommended, therefore, the influence of this policy was very limited since not all drugs had this identity.

New Round of Health Reform in China (2009–2010)

Along with the major healthcare reform in 2009, the Chinese government planned to invest 850 billion Yuan (approximately 124.26 billion US dollars) over the next 3 years to improve primary medical services and to make it more affordable. To further specify the healthcare reform, a series of policies were released from the national to the municipal level.

Different from the situation in the previous period, in which the application of EPR and drug tracking technologies were mostly based on bottom-up initiatives of hospitals and pharmaceutical firms, the developments after the announcement of a new round of healthcare reform showed a clear top-down structure.

[11] Sinopharm was a state-owned monopoly in the area of narcotics distribution till 2007, later on the Chinese government issued licenses to another two distributors in order to be in accordance with the Antitrust Act.

[12] The main concepts of GMP were developed in the United States. The GMP standards were introduced in China in 1980s, and until now the Chinese government has already modified them three times. The GSP standards were designed by SFDA.

EPR (Electronic Patient Records)

Although it had been almost 10 years since the first appearance of EPR in China, nearly no legislation existed to support the application of EPR before 2009. Progress was slowly made after the announcement of "Opinions of the State Council on Deepening the Healthcare System Reform", which symbolized the beginning of a new round of health reform:

- The draft of "The Basic Architecture and Data Standards of Electronic Patient Records (for trial implementation)" published by the Ministry of Health in 2009 aimed to make patient records more uniform and standardized.[13]
- In the "Basic Guidelines for Electronic Patient Records (for trial implementation)" issued in 2010, the Ministry of Health clarified the definition of EPR and its working guidelines.
- In 2010, the Ministry of Health released "Working Plans for the EPR Trial Implementation" to encourage the provincial and municipal governments to draft more localized guidelines in terms of EPR implementation; 22 out of all 23 provinces in China will start EPR trial implementation. The goal was to spread EPR throughout the country.
- To prevent the misuse of electronic patient records, the Ministry of Health further issued "Measures for Digital Certificates in the Healthcare Sector (for trial implementation)" in 2010, in which the relevant authority, responsibility and working guidelines were regulated.
- The Ministry of Health published a new version of "Basic Standards of Medical Records Writing" in 2010, which illustrated the detailed working processes involving EPR, supervision measures, and methods to secure patient information.

With nationwide trial implementations of EPR, the influence of government legislation clearly came to the fore. However, some challenges were also discovered during these trial implementations: (1) due to the unequal economic development in urban and rural areas, it was difficult to keep all EPRs maintained in hospitals on the same level of quality and detail; (2) the several EPR formats in use were not compatible, and it created a barrier for exchanging information among hospitals; (3) electronic patient records are collected in individual hospital information systems due to a lack of a centralized databank, which makes it difficult to share patient information on a national level. Standardization became a core issue for further expansion and progress of EPR.

Drug Tracking

As was mentioned before, the standardization of drug barcodes plays an essential role in drug tracking; the most important progress during this period was the appearance of the electronic supervision barcode released by SFDA, which

[13] Yu Yun 2010, Evaluation of E-health in China, 23rd Bled e-Conference, Slovenia.

provided a nationally standardized barcode for basic drugs.[14] According to "The Notice of Electronic Monitoring for the Basic Drug Catalogue" and the "Guidelines for Electronic Drug Monitoring Technologies" issued in 2010, adopting the SFDA supervision barcode became the prerequisite for basic medicines to be part of the centralized bidding process[15]; it was then possible to track basic drugs through the supervision barcode.

However, some disputes also arose around whether the introduction of a supervision barcode could be a solution to unify drug barcodes. Above all, the supervision barcode is not applied to all drugs and also not across the whole supply chain, hospitals and retailers were not obligated to adopt it because the SFDA does not have authority over medical institutes. Second, the government did not share detailed information about the supervision barcode, so pharmaceutical firms could not use it for internal management; as a result, they still use their own product codes for drug tracking.

Improvements in Legislation for EPR and Drug Tracking (2011–2012)

2011 marked the 3rd year of the new healthcare reform; it was reported that the government expenditures on public healthcare totaled 1.5 trillion Yuan over the past 3 years, which is 650 billion Yuan more than originally planned, and the Twelfth Five-Year Plan approved by the National People's Congress expresses the willingness of continued investments and the hope of consolidation within the industry. Numerous pilot projects started in different regions, including the "3521 Project" which aimed to implement hospital information systems in more than 420,000 village clinics in the central and western regions of China in order to achieve a balanced development between rural and urban areas.

EPR (Electronic Patient Records)

The Ministry of Health has released more detailed guidelines to support and to regulate the implementation of EPR:

- "Standards for EPR System Functions (for trial implementation)" presented the main functions of EPR systems as well as some recommendations.
- In the "Guidelines for EPR Evaluation", the Ministry of Health classified EPR performance into eight levels, so hospitals can better understand their current position and future developments.

[14] The Ministry of Health created a basic drug catalogue, which included 307 of the most used generic drugs in China. All low level hospitals like community hospitals, county hospitals, etc. must purchase drugs according to this basic drug catalogue.

[15] According to regulations, all state-owned, non-profit medical institutes must procure basic drugs through a centralized bidding process; the goal was to better control drug prices.

- "Technical Solutions to EPR-Based Hospital Information Platform Construction (Version 1.0)" is a central guideline for the construction of a hospital information system, provincial and municipal governments are also encouraged to draft detailed legislation based on local contexts.

At the end of 2011, more than 5.26 million electronic health records were established in Beijing; the Beijing Health Bureau requires all local secondary and tertiary hospitals to implement EPR by the end of 2014, and those electronic patient records should be accessible by different hospitals in 2015; patients in Fujian province can use one medical card for medical treatments in all public hospitals within the province; in some undeveloped regions where no hospital information system is implemented, medical institutes choose to have mutual recognition of examination results such as X-ray pictures and blood tests, which is seen as a preparation for future construction of EPR systems. Some preliminary progress is already seen today, whereas the issue of EPR standardization remains unresolved, which makes exchanging information among different hospitals impossible. Patients are also unable to receive reimbursements across different regions; furthermore, EPR application is still in an unstable phase, technology problems occur from time to time.[16]

Drug Tracking

Both the Ministry of Commerce and the Ministry of Industry and Information Technology have strongly proposed consolidation within the industry in the Twelfth Five-Year Plan. For this purpose, the government updated the GMP (Good Manufacturing Practice) and GSP (Good Sales Practice) standards to increase licensing requirements. Such consolidation could simplify the market structure by reducing the number of sales intermediaries involved in the pharmaceutical supply chain, and the path of drug tracking would be shortened.

The so far only existing national drug barcode, the Drug Supervision Barcode issued by the SFDA, was further developed over this period; it has been extended to all narcotics, blood products, vaccines and basic drugs till 2012. Furthermore, according to "A Notice of Electronic Drug Monitoring", some imported medicines are included in this list as well. Two-thirds of Chinese manufacturers are using the supervision barcode for 56,000 drugs, which represents 32 % of all drug varieties. Meanwhile, approximately 50,000 retail pharmacies joined the project and started to use the supervision barcode.[17] In the announcement of "Interim Measures for Drug Supervision and Management in Medical Institutions", the SFDA tried to persuade hospitals to implement the supervision barcode as well so that drugs can be tracked throughout the whole supply chain. However, since the SFDA doesn't have control over hospitals, as mentioned above, this guideline could only be recommended.

---

[16] Blog News, http://blog.sina.com.cn/u/1808556792.

[17] Blog News, http://blog.sina.com.cn/u/1808556792.

According to the latest guideline issued on October 9th 2012 by the SFDA, government will start to share more details about the supervision barcode with pharmaceutical firms so that the standardized drug barcode can also be used for company information systems.

Conclusion

Overall, it is clear from this appendix that China is making progress in implementing EPR systems as well as drug tracking technologies. However, a series of legislations which the Chinese government has issued during the healthcare reform had very limited success in their implementation.

The major challenge the government faces now is the lack of information technology standards caused by a large number of pharmaceutical firms and medical institutes, and the regional disparity in economic development. Together, these make data exchange tremendously complicated. Therefore, industry consolidation is strongly encouraged by the government which can create an easier environment to enforce governmental policies. The complexity of adopting EPR systems and drug tracking technologies in a fragmented industry structure requires adequate information exchange and further cooperation within and between government organizations and the healthcare industry.

A Timeline of EPR and Drug Tracking Development in China

	Politics & Legislation	EPR	Drug tracking
1992	SFDA adopted and modified the US. GMP standards, which included the definition and standards of drug batch number		
1994	An official of the Health Ministry raised the topic of EPR construction at the 6th Medical Informatics Conference, and it's hoped that there could be some pioneering hospitals to lead the trend		At the beginning of the 1990s, some large pharmaceutical companies and pharmacy retailers started to adopt ERP systems, which was a precondition for drug tracking
1998	"Measures for the Administration of Commodity Barcode", issued by General Administration of Quality Supervision		

(continued)

(continued)

	Politics & Legislation	EPR	Drug tracking
2001		The Appearance of EPR in China. First phase (2000–2002): The handwritten patient records were replaced by word or text format documents	Establishment of a national network for the narcotics supply chain, in which all narcotic records were collected
2003	"Development Plan of National ICT in the Healthcare Sector (2003–2010)", issued by the Ministry of Health	Second phase (2003–2007): EPR systems were developed separately from HIS systems; the user interface of EPR systems became more professional	
2005	The modified version of Measures for the Administration of Commodity Barcode, issued by the SFDA		
2005	"Electronic Signature Law" recognized the validity of electronic documents		
2007	Updated Supervision Guideline for Drug Distribution		
2008		Third phase (2008-present): EPR systems are integrated with HIS system	
2009	"Opinions of the State Council on Deepening the Healthcare System Reform" symbolized the beginning of a new round of healthcare reform		
2009	"The Implementation Plan of the Healthcare Reform from 2009 to 2011" indicated the working plans for the next 3 years		
2009	"The Basic Architecture and Data Standards of Electronic Patient Records (for trial implementation)" drafted by the Ministry of Health revealed more details of EPR standardization		

(continued)

(continued)

	Politics & Legislation	EPR	Drug tracking
2010	"Basic Guidelines for Electronic Patient Records (for trial implementation)" clarified the definition and the working guidelines of EPR		
2010	The Ministry of Health released "The Notice of EPR (for trial implementation)" to encourage the provincial and municipal governments to draft more localized guidelines in terms of EPR implementation. The goal was to spread EPR throughout the country	EPR pilot implementation took place in more than 22 provinces	
2010	The "Notice of Electronic Monitoring for the Basic Drug Catalogue", issued by SFDA		All pharmaceutical companies are asked to adopt supervision barcodes on the smallest unit of drug packaging in order to take part in the centralized drug bidding process
2010	"Guidelines for Electronic Drug Monitoring Technologies"		
2010	To prevent the misuse of electronic patient Records, the Ministry of Health further issued "Measures for Digital Certificates in the Healthcare Sector (for trial implementation)", in which authority, responsibility and working guidelines are regulated		
2010	The Ministry of Health passed a new version of "Basic Standards of Medical Records Writing", which illustrate the working details with EPR, supervision measures and information security etc		

(continued)

(continued)

	Politics & Legislation	EPR	Drug tracking
2011	"12th Five-Year Plan"		
2011	New GMP Standard, issued by SFDA		
2011	New GSP Standard, issued by SFDA		
2011	"Standardized Functions of EPR System (for trial implementation)" presented the main functions of EPR systems as well as some recommendations	At the end of 2011, more than 5,26 million electronic health records were established in Beijing; Beijing Health Bureau required all local secondary and tertiary hospitals to implement EPR by the end of 2014, and those electronic patient records are supposed to be able to share among different hospitals in 2005; patients in Fujian province can use one medical card for medical treatments in all public hospitals within the province; in some undeveloped regions where no hospital information system is implemented, medical institutes choose to have mutual recognition of examination results e.g. X-ray picture and blood test etc., which is seen as a preparation for future construction of EPR	
2011	EPR systems are evaluated and classified into eight levels according to the " Guidelines for EPR Evaluation", so hospitals can better understand their current position and pursue future developments		
2011	"Technical Solutions to EPR-Based Hospital Information Platform Construction (Version 1.0)" is a central guideline for the construction of a hospital information system		
2011	In the announcement of the "Interim Measures for Drug Supervision and Management in Medical Institutions", the SFDA tried to persuade hospitals to implement the supervision barcode as well, so that drugs can be tracked throughout the whole supply chain		Hospital presidents showed their willingness to cooperate with commercial companies in terms of HIS and drug Tracking & Tracing. The topics of drug tracking and standardization of drug codes have been frequently discussed in all kinds of industry conference, yet no agreement has been achieved

(continued)

(continued)

	Politics & Legislation	EPR	Drug tracking
2012	"Work Plan for Electronic Drug Monitoring in 2011-2015", issued by SFDA		(1) Till Feb 2012, the national supervision barcode has covered all narcotics, blood products, vaccines, and basic drug category etc., which means 2/3 of Chinese manufacturers are using supervision barcode for about 56,000 drugs (32 % of the all drug varieties.) (2) About 50,000 pharmacy retailers have also adopted supervision barcode, further expansion is expected
2012	According to "A Notice of Electronic Drug Monitoring", the imported medicines are also required to have supervision barcodes		
2012	"A Working Guidance for Electronic Drug Monitoring (Trial)", SFDA		
2012	According to the latest guideline issued on October 9th 2012 by the SFDA, government will start to share more details about the supervision barcode with pharmaceutical firms so that the standardized drug barcode can also be used for internal information systems		

SpringerBriefs on Digital Spaces

SpringerBriefs on Digital Spaces is an international research program—the ISD—launched in 2009 by the CIGREF Foundation (www.fondation-cigref.org). The series aims at making a set of concepts, ideas and results of projects carried out under the program available to the research, business and policy communities. ISD—Information Systems Dynamics, is a research program of public interest that works to evaluate the societal and managerial challenges related to the long-term use of information systems and digitality.

Since its launch in 2009, the program has already supported more than 30 projects conducted by international teams from different academic backgrounds (Computer Science, Management Science, Economics, Sociology, Geography and Anthropology) as well as from different geographical regions (Europe, North America and Asia).

The program works on the premise that the *spatial dimension* of the use of digital systems and artefacts is a critical perspective for understanding the dynamics of value creation—and more generally of socio-economizing—in our economies and societies. Understanding emerging practices in digital spaces is a key step toward delineating and conceptualizing a substantial part of the emerging paradigms of economic activities in the 21st century. *Springer Briefs in Digital Spaces* publishes research findings and monographs related to the different facets of these issues. By doing so, the series seeks to contribute to the necessary dialogue between the researchers, practitioners and public policymakers involved in these very critical and rapidly changing fields of research and action.

Editor

The series is edited by Ahmed Bounfour, Professor, European Chair on Intellectual Capital Management, University Paris-Sud, and General Rapporteur of the ISD program.

K. Reimers et al., *Innovating in a Learning Community*, SpringerBriefs in Digital Spaces, DOI: 10.1007/978-3-319-05098-0, © The Author(s) 2014

MIX
Papier aus verantwortungsvollen Quellen
Paper from responsible sources
FSC® C105338

If you have any concerns about our products,
you can contact us on
ProductSafety@springernature.com

In case Publisher is established outside the EU,
the EU authorized representative is:
Springer Nature Customer Service Center GmbH
Europaplatz 3, 69115 Heidelberg, Germany

Printed by Libri Plureos GmbH
in Hamburg, Germany